Praise for
Warrior Goddess Training

"HeatherAsh Amara is a woman who I love and treasure. Her honesty and integrity is on every page of *Warrior Goddess Training*. HeatherAsh is your coach and impeccable teacher in the life-ceremony that is offered in this book. Using the effective steps in *Warrior Goddess Training,* you can work through the layers of 'sick and tired,' boredom, and suffocating conditioning. The result? You will finally be able to connect with yourself and others, and live as your precious wild self."

—Ana Tiger Forrest, medicine woman,
creatrix of Forrest Yoga, and
author of *Fierce Medicine*

"Sisters, its time to shed the . . . ourselves through our own eyes instead of others, and close the gap between wishing for and realizing once and for all who we came here to be. No one shows you how to walk this journey with courage and compassionate self-acceptance better than gifted teacher HeatherAsh Amara. If you are ready to discover who you really are and support becoming your best self, pick up this book and get started today. The world needs your light now!"

—Stephanie Bennett Vogt,
author of *Your Spacious Self*

"This is a book for all women, no matter their age or stage of life. HeatherAsh Amara is a master teacher who embodies the concepts of *warrior* and *goddess* in her life and writing. For me, the line in the book that most reflects the lessons a woman can learn from her is this: 'Being a Warrior Goddess is about falling in love with *all* of yourself.' Each lesson she presents offers insight and practices for spiritual, physical, intellectual, and psychological growth and refinement. HeatherAsh's openness about her own journey of becoming a Warrior Goddess adds a sense of authenticity and lightness to the book."

—Judith Yost, Dean of Students,
Wisdom School of Graduate Studies and
author of *Nature and Intimacy*

WARRIOR GODDESS TRAINING

HEATHERASH AMARA

Hierophant publishing

Cover design by Adrian Morgan
Cover art by Elena Ray
Interior design by Jane Hagaman
Author Photo by Nicholas Rozsa

Hierophant Publishing
8301 Broadway, Suite 219
San Antonio, TX 78209
888-800-4240
www.hierophantpublishing.com

If you are unable to order this book from your local bookseller, you may order directly from the publisher.

Library of Congress Control Number: 2014943956

ISBN 978-1-938289-36-1

15 14 13 12 11

Printed on acid-free paper in the United States of America

This book is dedicated to all the women on this beautiful planet. May we reclaim the fierce love of the warrior and embody the wisdom of the goddess to bring balance and harmony to the Earth.

There came a time when the risk to remain tight in the bud was more painful than the risk it took to blossom.

—Anaïs Nin

Contents

Foreword

In *Warrior Goddess Training*, HeatherAsh Amara shares her experience as a teacher, friend, and guide, helping a new generation of women enter their own journey of inner transformation.

This book combines the wisdom of many traditions into one beautiful path. Consistent throughout these teachings is the understanding that an idea means nothing without a corresponding step toward action; therefore, this book is full of exercises that are designed to put you in touch with your divine self.

As you will soon see, the path of the Warrior Goddess was forged in love.

HeatherAsh Amara came into my life over twenty years ago as a college student who had so many questions about everything; so many that she took on many teachers in many traditions, including myself, and began her trek toward understanding. At first she wanted to understand everything that existed outside of herself, but all of her teachers pointed inward. So when her resistance to this direction ended, her trek to outward understanding turned into a journey of self-understanding. The pages that follow are the result of that journey.

The path of the Warrior Goddess is described in ten lessons. The first three lessons will help you center yourself and assess where you are, the next six lessons will guide you through a path of personal transformation, and the final lesson invites you to live your truth as a Warrior Goddess in your everyday life.

I am incredibly happy to see that the young girl who walked into my class over twenty years ago has not only become a radiant a woman, a teacher, an author, and a Warrior Goddess, but most importantly, she has become an expression of unconditional love.

With this great work of art, let the words and teachings of this artist guide you to your own divine self and the blossoming of unconditional love in your heart. This is the journey of love that is the Warrior Goddess path.

In the Toltec tradition, the last step before an apprentice becomes a master is when the student lets go of the teacher as a crutch for support and learns to walk with the strength of her own will. The traces of her teacher's lessons may remain with subsequent steps, but what shines through is the wisdom of her own experiences. HeatherAsh Amara was once my apprentice, and now she is my peer.

Thank you, HeatherAsh Amara, for birthing this wonderful book.

—don Miguel Ruiz,
author of *The Four Agreements*
and *The Mastery of Love*

Preface

I was called to work with women many years ago, when I took my first college class called Women and Society and began to explore Earth-based spirituality.

Earth-based spirituality is any religion or tradition that at its center honors the Earth, nature, and all manifestations of life. Practiced by people all over the world, from Native American tribes to African shamans to modern-day scientists, Earth-based spirituality views the Earth as the Mother, the one who gives us life and nourishment and brings insight and wisdom.

Connected to the cycles of the Earth and sun, these traditional teachings honor light and dark, beginnings and endings, male and female, birth and death. Everything is included; all is sacred. As I immersed myself in studying different traditions, I found a deep sense of home in European shamanism and its teachings on honoring Mother Earth. The archetypes of maiden, mother, and crone and the different aspects of the Goddess inspired me to begin to love myself as a woman, rather than trying to be more like the male God and people (mostly men) who were held up as role models and guides.

In time I found teachers to guide me, and I was "drafted" to teach by the sheer number of women who kept coming to me, asking to learn. As women, we crave a female reflection of the Divine, and a spirituality that empowers us to connect to our natural gifts of intuition, healing, and building community. This has nothing to do with being better than men, or wanting to lead separate lives from our brothers, or being special because of our biology. It is about honoring all of life: female and male, human and animal, plant and mineral. And it is about the magic that happens when we gather to empower ourselves as women, and to honor and be inspired by all the manifestations of the goddess in each other.

This book was birthed out of a year-long program I created in 1997 called Thirteen Moons, named for the thirteen new moon cycles in a year. Thirteen Moons was first inspired by my first two female teachers, Vicki Noble and Cerridwen Fallingstar, whom I apprenticed with. During that time, I filled up on the nourishment of women gathering together to unconditionally support each other.

Through Vicki I learned about the ancestral wisdom of women's intuition, healing, and amazing strength; through Cerridwen I was opened to intimacy and vulnerability with my sisters, aligning with the cycles of the seasons, and the healing gift of ritual. Thirteen Moons was also nourished by a small circle of my heart sisters from college, the Women of Yes, that met every week.

The transformative heart of Thirteen Moons came through my long Toltec apprenticeship and teaching partnership with don Miguel Ruiz, author of *The Four Agreements*. The Toltec were a group of ancient people who chose to come together in South and Central Mexico over one thousand years ago. They considered themselves "artists of the spirit." As don Miguel writes: "Find yourself and express yourself in your own particular way. Express your love openly. Life is nothing but a dream, and if you create your life with love, your dream becomes a masterpiece of art."

After three years of ardent study, I was able to integrate the core teachings of European shamanism and Toltec wisdom into my everyday life. I found a powerful balance of the two with the Thirteen Moons program, and I began teaching women this blend of Toltec warrior philosophy and European goddess spirituality to empower them to create positive change in their own lives.

And wow, did it work. In the first year of the program I witnessed sixteen women blossom like wildflowers after the spring rains. Within a circle that said YES to personal truth and authenticity, each woman pushed through the weeds of self-doubt and claimed her path. From finishing old projects to starting new careers, from clearing stuck parental patterns to starting a family, from healing sexual trauma to reclaiming her passion for life, each woman thrived.

From this first circle Thirteen Moons grew into an apprenticeship circle for women around the world. Our global hub via the Web reaches across all borders to connect women in busy cities and isolated towns to a circle that blasts open the doors of possibility and self-love.

Warrior Goddess Training is the newest expression of the Thirteen Moons teachings, simmered over years of experience and distilled in ten potently simple lessons. May they nourish your heart and soul to blossom as the Warrior Goddess that you are.

While I am the mama that birthed the initial form of Thirteen Moons and now *Warrior Goddess Training*, the teachings are from our grandmothers, our grandmothers' grandmothers, passed down verbally, recreated and reinvented by modern grandmothers and mothers for all women. I especially honor Madre Sarita, don Miguel's mother, for the many ways she has guided me in bringing the Toltec lineage teachings forward, even after her death.

Introduction

*I don't want to get to the end of my life
and find that I lived just the length of it. I
want to have lived the width of it as well.*

—Diane Ackerman

You are whole. You are powerful. You are divine.

When you read these words do you feel the truth of them ringing in your bones? I feel empowered! powerful

Or do you instead feel the muffling weight of self-judgment and self-doubt? Perhaps you have a deep-seated belief that you are not good enough, and as a result you have tried the exhausting process of seeking value outside of yourself throughout your life.

If you don't love and honor yourself with every fiber of your being, if you struggle with owning your power and passion, if you could use more joyful play and simple presence in your life, then it is time for an inner revolution. It is time to claim your Warrior Goddess energy.

As women, we are trained to seek our wholeness and value and to find love through others. Fifty years ago, we were told a husband and children would complete us—that was about our only option. Today, what makes us worthy might be a beloved, our career, or even following a chosen spiritual path. We rarely see ourselves as perfect just the way we are. We often base our worth on who loves or doesn't love us, if we need to lose that extra five or fifty pounds, and if we can juggle three tasks simultaneously while keeping a smile on our face.

The new women's revolution is an evolution from being other-focused to inner-focused. When our attention is trapped by fearful shoulds, what ifs, and don'ts, we scatter our energy and struggle with knowing what is authentic for us. When we bring our attention back to discovering who we are on the inside—not who we wish we were or who we think we should be—we begin a sacred path of transformation toward our innate, authentic, embodied power.

This is the path of the Warrior Goddess.

Warrior energy is a combination of focus, dedication, purpose, and determination. Consciously bringing these things together gives us our power. When we harness our warrior energy we are confident, clear, and bring 100 percent of ourselves to each action.

Goddess energy is our creative flow: unconditional love, pleasure, passion, and wisdom. When we claim our goddess energy we live in joyful self-acceptance and self-respect, and we listen to our sacred inner voice.

So let's start at the beginning.

The irony is that the first step on this path is not about gaining some insight or attaining a new state of being. Rather, it requires you to relinquish some things that you have been holding on to for a long, long time. On a path of transformation, you must be willing to give up your false beliefs and self-limiting stories.

A story is something we tell ourselves and others to explain why we are the way we are. Our stories may be of inspiration, or woe and blame. Our stories might fill us with energy and enthusiasm, or make us feel helpless and victimized or angry and defensive. The stories we tell that limit our expression and joy are filled with false beliefs and attachments that really do not serve us. The question to ask is this: Is my story causing internal and external drama, or is it bringing me peace and fulfillment?

Those inner voices that say "I am not smart enough," "I am not pretty enough," or "I am not outgoing enough" are the false ideas that are the bedrock for the limiting belief structure we hold. Many of us have been telling ourselves these stories for so long we no longer recognize them as stories; we accept them as facts. But nothing could be further from the truth!

If you are ready to stop clinging to your limitations, the first step is to let go of the belief that you are a victim or a martyr. If you view yourself as powerless and helpless, or believe you need to be something you are not to be accepted, these stories will rule your life and define your reality.

It is time to remove any mask or protective shell you are hiding behind to fully experience the world. You must be willing to openhandedly release the past and surrender up the future. Most importantly, *you must be willing to give up who you think you should be in favor of who you are.*

Let's get you ready to be your beautiful, powerful self.

In the mythic story of the hero, a single man ventures out to find his fortune, combat evil, save a woman or two, and demonstrate his strength against all obstacles.

In the modern story of the heroine Warrior Goddess, a single woman ventures out to find herself, combat fear and doubt, reclaim her power and vibrancy, and demonstrate her strength of compassion and fierce love.

As twenty-first-century heroines, we have a cornucopia of obstacles to overcome and lots of demons to slay on our journey to release our true self. We live in a time when stress, self-loathing, self-abuse, and addiction are normal, and where sexual, emotional, and physical abuse are all too prevalent. And while we are blessed that our grandmothers and mothers laid a pathway for women's liberation and personal freedom in the outside world by fighting for things like the right to vote, equal treatment at the workplace, and so on, many of us are still chained by trying to live up to standards, beliefs, and ideals that are not our own.

Warrior Goddess Training is about finding out who you really are and what you really want, and, armed with that knowledge, creating an external reality that authentically matches who you are on the inside.

As authors Carrie McCarthy and Danielle LaPorte write in their book, *Style Statements*, life starts to get problematically dull when we fail to look within, when we lose touch with our own sense of what feels right or wrong. When we feed ourselves a diet of ideas about success and happiness that other people have cooked up, then our genuine character begins to starve and we make weak choices about what we bring into our lives and put out into the world.

The shift from being other-focused to being inner-focused takes courage. It is easier to follow what we know, to stay safe in the familiar. But on the path of the Warrior Goddess, there is no one-size-fits-all template, no mold to follow, no get-out-of-jail-free card, no white knight to save you, and no realized master or loving guru or powerful shaman who will instantly awaken you to who you really are. This is one journey you will make alone, but, surrounded by supportive sisters and brothers, you will turn to face inward, clearing out any debris, noise, stagnation, or dullness to reveal the radiant jewel of you.

The good news is that it's never too late to become the real you. That's what the planet needs at this moment: you, 100 percent.

All around the world, women are stepping forward to invite back their authentic, creative, wonderfully unique selves. We are shedding the old, faded clothes of war, domination, competition, jealousy, and repression. We are rising like the sun, shining big and bright as the full moon. We are saying yes to the power of fierce love, compassion, constant authenticity, and vulnerability. These are the attributes of our warrior focus and our goddess joy.

Reclaiming this feminine authenticity doesn't make us more evolved than men, or better than our sisters who are living from their domestication rather than their essence. As humans we are all equal, all precious.

We are all whole. Sometimes we just get so lost in the fog of our own self-limiting beliefs that we need a guide to lead us back to the light of unconditional self-love and self-acceptance. This book is just such a guide.

Returning to the Circle

For thousands of years, in tribes and villages around the world women have come together in circles to share, to teach, to listen, to learn. The pulse of these women still beats within us. Their wisdom flows through time, whispering to us the song of female connection and beauty. We only need to stop long enough and put our ear to our heart to hear the call.

One beautiful example of women coming together for healing and learning was the moon lodge. As Native American clan mother Spider writes in her book, *Songs of Bleeding*: When women started to bleed, they left their homes and families to go to the sacred introspective space of the Bleeding Lodge. The Lodge was honored and respected by the entire community, for the dreams and visions of the bleeding women brought vital survival information such as planting and healing knowledge and guidance on community relations. When there were questions that needed to be answered, the women would go to the Lodge and ask the Ancestors.

It was here, in retreat from daily life, that the wisdom of women was passed down and new insights and visions were shared for the benefit of the entire community. While many of these ancient ancestral teachings have been lost, they live within us still.

I see the wisdom of our grandmothers as a seed we each inherit at birth, patiently waiting to be unearthed and opened. This is our heritage, a coming home to ourselves and our circle.

As Starhawk, author of *The Spiral Dance* and one of the main inspirations behind the Goddess movement, writes,

> We are all longing to go home to some place we have never been—a place half-remembered and half-envisioned we can only catch glimpses of from time to time. Community. Somewhere, there are people to whom we can speak with passion without having the words catch in our throats. Somewhere a circle of hands will open to receive us, eyes will light up as we enter, voices will celebrate with us whenever we come into our own power. Community means strength that joins our strength to do the work that needs to be done. Arms to hold us when we falter. A circle of healing. A circle of friends. Someplace where we can be free.

This book represents a sacred gathering of women healing, laughing, and growing. Within these pages you will discover the lessons of the Warrior Goddess. Each chapter is a pathway of discovery, awakening, and reconnection to your female roots and community. Each word invites you to become the woman you are meant to be.

The first three Warrior Goddess lessons are foundational, designed to help you commit, align, and purify your being. The next six lessons are transformational, a guided journey to clean and vitalize the main aspects of yourself. The final lesson is inspirational, encouraging you to bring your light more fully into the world.

Each lesson is designed to help you shed the dull skin of old patterns and habits and emerge as the Warrior Goddess who is waiting within. Each lesson also offers hands-on practice you can sink your teeth into to continue the transformation in your inner and outer worlds. Many chapters begin with a personal story about the places I've struggled and the insights I've gained, the spectacular stumbles and the picking myself up and moving on. I do not pretend to be enlightened, spiritually advanced, or complete in my learning. I consider myself a determined Warrior and a sassy Goddess, a fabulous work in progress. I'm a woman, like you, learning, growing, laughing, and crying. I make mistakes. I step on people's toes. I get caught in fear and self-doubt. I still take things personally. Sometimes I feel invincible, sometimes I feel fragile and vulnerable. I honor and cherish all these parts of myself—even the ones I don't like so much. I hope that by the end of this book, you will also love your mistakes, laugh at your fears, have faith in yourself, and know the rich support of your sisters.

For additional support, at the end of the book you'll find a Further Reading section which lists supplemental books you can consult as you're working your way through each lesson. I also encourage you to connect with other Warrior Goddesses on your journey, so the Resources section lists all the places you can go on the Web to find other *Warrior Goddess Training* readers around the world, plus additional resources for each Warrior Goddess lesson.

I'm excited and honored to be on this journey with you, a journey of claiming our fierce warrior self and embracing our divine feminine goddess greatness. May you open this door to yourself with the delight of a child unwrapping the gift they wanted most. The love, faith, and integrity you have been seeking await you. Let's begin by taking a moment to connect to all women around the world. Tap into the love of our female ancestors. Breathing in, draw in the strength and wisdom of the abundance of Warrior Goddess kick-ass females throughout the ages. Breathing out, release old ways of being to make space for your intuition, insight, and loving fierceness to emerge.

And now make a commitment to be fully, 100 percent YOU.

You are whole. You are valued. You are loved.

I see your wholeness.

I know your value.

I love you, just the way you are.

Welcome to the path of the Warrior Goddess.

Explanation of Key Terms

Before we begin this journey together. I want to explain some key terms I will use throughout this book to make sure we're all on the same page.

Agreements—Anytime we say yes to a belief or way of being, even if we are doing so unconsciously, we are making an agreement. Agreements can serve us, like when we make an agreement to stop eating food our body doesn't like, or they can hurt us, like when we accept other people's erroneous opinions as fact (racism and sexism are easy examples of this). Agreements can also be made consciously or unconsciously. A conscious agreement might be a contract you sign, a promise you make, or a goal you set. An unconscious agreement might be never singing or dancing because your mom or dad never sang or danced. When we are conscious of our agreements we can make better choices about which ones serve us and which ones we want to release.

Attachment—When we have an expectation or desire for how people, things, or events should be, we have an attachment. When we are highly attached we are grasping on to something outside of ourselves to feel safe. The stronger the expectation, the deeper the attachment, and the more we suffer when it is not met or when it goes away. As humans we naturally attach to things that we love: other people, our houses, our pets. We also attach to things to define our self-worth: our youth, our job, our intelligence. As we find more stability and peace within, our external attachments start to fall away, and we are filled with more unconditional love and acceptance than fear, even when change happens.

Domestication—In the context of this book, domestication expresses the Toltec idea of how we are conditioned by the society in which we live. It's how we are taught to behave or to fit in, usually by the reward of acceptance or the punishment of withheld love. While domestication is important to pass on the framework and rules of the society we are born into, it often creates an internal split between who we are and who we are told we should be. When we choose to be what others want us to be, we end up being dissatisfied with our life, because we are not living from our authenticity, but from our domestication.

Earth Goddess Spirituality—Religion offers a scripture and a structure, a place of refuge in the form of a building and a community where we come together to celebrate the teachings of a prophet or culture. Spirituality is a conscious personal connection to the Divine, as varied as each individual. Earth spirituality treats the Earth, the elements (such as air, fire, water, earth) and the cycles of life as sacred and views God not as an outside being, but as the creative force that is immanent within all things. Goddess spirituality praises and takes inspiration from the reflection of the feminine divine, which is sometimes manifest in an all-compassionate figure, such as Kuan Yin from China, Mother Mary from Europe, and the Virgin of Guadalupe from Mexico, and is sometimes portrayed as a ferocious destroyer of illusion, such as Kali from India or Hecate from Europe.

Most Goddess traditions from around the world do not exclude the masculine, but see the divine principle as the Mother who unconditionally loves all her children, male and female. Riane Eisler, author of *The Chalice and the Blade*, sums this up well:

> Data from Catal Huyuk and other Neolithic sites also indicate that in these societies, where women were priestesses and craftspeople, the female was not subordinate to the male. Although the sacred union of female and male was an important religious mystery, the powers that create and govern the universe were generally depicted as a goddess rather than a god.

European Shamanism—Pre-Christian, Earth-based spirituality flourished in what is now the British Isles and the continent of Europe. Shamanism is a global phenomenon that predates all major religions around the world, and it is a practice of direct revelation and healing through journeying and communing with nature. Sandra Ingerman, author of many books, including *Soul Retrieval: Mending the Fragmented Self* and *Yearning for the Wind: Celtic Reflections on Nature and the Soul*, writes:

> Shamanism teaches us that everything that exists is alive and has a spirit. Shamans speak of a web of life that connects all of life and the spirit that lives in all things. Everything on Earth is interconnected and any belief that we are separate from other life forms including the Earth, stars, wind, etc. is

purely an illusion. And it is the shaman's role in the community to keep harmony and balance between humankind and the forces of nature.

European shamanism honors the four elements of air, fire, water, and earth; the cycles of the seasons and life; and in some traditions the triple Goddess: maiden, mother, and crone.

Toltec people and Toltec philosophy—The Toltec were an ancient group of indigenous people who came together over one thousand years ago in south and central Mexico to study perception. They are the builders of the pyramids in Teotihuacán, Mexico. After the Spanish conquest of Mexico, the Toltec teachings continued to be shared in secret, often passed down through families. The first Toltec teachings to reappear to a large audience were the teachings of Don Juan, through anthropologist Carlos Castaneda. Castaneda's many books, including *Journey to Ixtlan* and *Tales of Power*, inspired thousands of people to begin to incorporate Toltec wisdom into their lives. Author and teacher don Miguel Ruiz brought the wisdom of the Toltec to an even wider audience with his *New York Times* best-selling books *The Four Agreements* and *The Mastery of Love*. In the latter book, Ruiz writes, Toltec knowledge arises from the same essential unity of truth as all the sacred esoteric traditions found around the world. Though it is not a religion, it honors all the spiritual masters who have taught on the Earth. While it does embrace spirit, it is most accurately described as a way of life, distinguished by the ready accessibility of happiness and love. The word *Toltec* means "artist of the spirit."

Commit to You

Don't ever give up.

Don't ever give in.

Don't ever stop trying.

Don't ever sell out.

And if you find yourself succumbing to one of the above for a brief moment,

pick yourself up, brush yourself off, whisper a prayer, and start where you left off.

But never, ever, ever give up.

—Richelle E. Goodrich

Most women know all about commitment. We commit to hiding or exaggerating our flaws, trying to make others happy or comfortable at the expense of our happiness and comfort, supporting other people's dreams at the expense of our own dreams, or criticizing ourselves (and others) at every turn. We commit to who we think we *should* be rather than committing to meeting ourselves where we are. We commit to seeing ourselves through other people's eyes, gauging our self-worth based on their acceptance, rather than witnessing our unique inner beauty and strength. We commit to being nice rather than being real, or we commit to being right rather than being vulnerable. And when people in our lives don't behave the way we think they should, we sulk and mope, or worse, we get even. We justify our emotional outbursts or bad behavior based on the actions of others, and in so doing we often act in the same manner as the person who set us off in the first place. When we give others the power to push our emotional buttons, we become their slaves, often without realizing it. The problem is, we are the ones who suffer.

Our first Warrior Goddess lesson, Commit to You, is designed to close the gap between self-rejection and true acceptance, thinking and being, wishing and becoming.

This commitment to self shows us that there is no hidden treasure or savior outside of ourselves; we *are* the treasure we have been searching for. Or, put another way, we are the one we have been waiting for.

Your commitment to this idea is the activation of your Warrior Goddess power. When your words, thoughts, and actions foster self-abuse and self-judgment, you are using your immense power against yourself. This type of emotional, mental, and physical denial can take many forms: saying yes when you really mean no, being in relationships that don't nourish you, thinking and believing thoughts that drain your energy and enthusiasm, eating foods your body doesn't like.

Committing to your true, authentic, Warrior Goddess self is the beginning of a lifelong journey of living in authenticity.

As I've worked to release the old habits of "I need-to-make-sure-everyone-likes-me or I need-to-be-saved" matrices within me, I've been amazed at times by how deeply the patterning has been woven through my being. I've been walking this path for over twenty years, yet life inevitably presents new and unexpected changes, and each such circumstance is an invitation for me to look within and release whatever is still holding me back. Like layers of an onion, there is more to be peeled, and each peeling is sometimes accompanied by a fresh shedding of tears. But every time I am willing to look within I am so grateful for every experience, every obstacle, every learning, because I've learned to use everything that arises in my field of awareness as a tool to discover who I truly am.

The keystone of committing to yourself is very simple: Learn to love all of who you are, flaws and all. Doing this, however, can be a difficult thing. You commit to yourself to the same extent that you are willing to release the past and any ideas that you are holding that you "should" be different than you are at this moment. Our deepest healing occurs when we learn to be our own best friend, companion, and cheerleader.

For example, the year my book *The Toltec Path of Transformation* was published was a pivotal point in my life that showed me what commitment to self really means. The same week my book was released my husband, teaching partner, and business partner moved out and headed for Colorado. I felt like someone had handed me a beautiful 160-page creation after months of hard labor, and then chopped off one of my legs. I didn't know how to stop the bleeding or how I was going to share the teachings in my book and feed my business and community when I felt so much loss.

Luckily, the book I had just written became a guide to remind me of the steps to freedom. I had written the perfect book at the perfect time; I just didn't realize I had written it for myself. As I reread the first paragraphs of *The Toltec Path of Transformation*, I simultaneously cursed, cried, and laughed.

Here is what I had written in the introduction:

Have you ever had your world turned upside down in an instant?

Or struggled to re-align with a big change in your life?

Or wished that some aspect of your life would shift?

Being in a physical form means that you are constantly invited to adjust to change, whether joyous or frightening. From your first lost tooth to your first heartbreak, from a child's graduation to the loss of a friend, from starting a new job to adjusting to a chronic illness, life continues to flow and sometimes gently, sometimes abruptly alter the landscape of your being.

How you adapt to the changes in your life can mean the difference between being in struggle and fear or in sweet ease and faith. The simple truth is that when you fight change you suffer. When you embrace change you open to creativity, possibility, and healing.

Change is inevitable, but transformation is by conscious choice. While you do not always have control over how or when the changes will occur in your life, you can choose how you are in relation to those changes. When you step towards rather than ignore, fight, or resist change, you reclaim your personal freedom. You step onto a path of transformation, and move from being a victim of change to being a co-creator with change.

Damn, I thought. The Universe was giving me yet another, deeper, opportunity to "walk the talk."

So there I stood, sobbing in my kitchen, missing my friend and lover. The house felt empty, as if all the comfort and joy had been drained from it. I vacillated between numb desert-island shock and drowning oceanic grief.

And then suddenly my mind cleared, and a point of clarity arose like a star on the horizon through the rolling storm of my emotions. I heard myself say, "What do you miss about him?"

Somehow I was able to let go of all the stories and sadness and bring my full attention to this simple question. What *did* I miss about him?

I internally scrolled through countless images and feelings of our ten years of living, teaching, and working together. What I was grieving in that moment was his quiet, calm love and presence.

In a flash I realized that I had two choices: I could spend years longing for something that was no longer present, or I could make a new Warrior Goddess commitment to myself.

As the waves of grief threatened to engulf me again, I took my Warrior Goddess power back.

"OK, sweetie," I said out loud to myself, "What are you going to do to bring what you are missing—quiet, calm love—into this space? How can you create that for yourself?"

As I looked around my house, I smiled. I knew it was time for me to stop looking outside myself for quiet, calm love, and to creatively commit to cultivating what I was craving. Over the next six months I externally cleared clutter and rearranged furniture, internally slowed down, increased my meditating, and practiced being more calmly loving to myself and others.

I also did a lot more grieving and had some spectacular emotional meltdowns. But at the end of each of these episodes, I recommitted to creating quiet, calm love in myself that I so desperately needed. Over time, the feelings of sadness and grief were released from my being, and I realized that this change in my life circumstances was exactly what I needed. My life was better because of it.

The point I want to make with this example is that when we commit to ourselves, we don't get to bypass our emotions or get a free "all-problems-go-away-instantly" pass. We don't magically change into the perfect person we've been judging ourselves for not being. Walking the Warrior Goddess path is a process, one that starts with the commitment to empower ourselves and continues to ask us to recommit to our healing and truth every time we face a new and often unexpected challenge.

Each time we recommit to ourselves, things change on the inside. We begin a process of realigning ourselves to our authentic power, and holding ourselves in a new way.

Let's look at old and new definitions of power, and how to use the first Warrior Goddess lesson to strengthen your commitment to yourself.

Attuning to a New Power

When you watch television or read magazines, what is most reflected in pictures and words is this: Power is defined by how you look, how much money you make, who you are dating/married to, and how you are progressing on your career track.

From a framework of fear and scarcity, powerful people are the ones who have, in one way or another, acquired the most sought-after or "best" external resources available, be that money, fame, or beauty.

Many of us have spent years tied to this old model of power, where we rate our worth on how we are perceived or what we have attained.

As women we worry about how others see our body, constantly asking ourselves: Are we pretty enough? Thin enough? Sexy enough? Since many of us have used our sexuality as a tool to get what we thought we wanted, we worry about getting older and no longer being attractive.

The same can be said for money and social status. We may worry we don't have the financial means to do everything thing we want to do, or that others don't recognize how important we are (through our own career accomplishments or those of our significant other's).

We struggle with our judgments around where we should be in our career or even on our spiritual path. We compare ourselves to others. We slip into jealousy and fear around other women who shine more brightly or threaten our sense of self in any way.

Even after we have acquired some of the things we think we want, our struggle with power is still not over. We then try to hold or increase our power by working to please others and control the outcome of situations, or we stay safe by hiding in the background and conforming to the status quo, hoping no one notices the power we have (and therefore cannot take it away).

When we don't acquire or hold on to the things valued by the old methods of power, we then resort to self-judgment and condemnation, saying that if we were only prettier, smarter, more dedicated, etc., then we would have everything we wanted and life would be full of bliss.

It is only when we begin to look at the old power structures in this way that we can see the insanity behind it.

From a Warrior Goddess point of view, power is defined very differently. Power is not sought after from the outside, but rather is patiently cultivated from within. Power has nothing to do with money, or fame, or outside appearances, but with our connection to self, love, authenticity, and the inner mystery of life. From the perspective of true abundance and immanent spiritual connection, powerful people are the ones who have the strongest connection to their internal resources.

Our challenge, then, is to be honest with the places we are still pursuing the old modes of power and to move ourselves toward attuning with a new power: our own. This will not be done all at once, but over time as we unhook ourselves from old patterns and agreements, consciously reconnecting to our authentic center.

Remember, becoming aware of where we have pursued the old methods of power is not a call for more self-judgment, but rather an opportunity to release these habits and recommit to our Warrior Goddess self. As we become more aware of what agreements, or beliefs, we are holding that don't serve us, we can choose again, can make conscious agreements that support and nourish who we really are.

Outside, the societal dream beckons us to buy more things, to stay young, to be in a relationship, to climb the career ladder, to have a child or two, to be sex kittens one second and sweet virgins the next. Inherently, none of these things are bad. But when we use them to fill up a feeling of emptiness within, or do them to please others rather than ourselves, they become our jail. When we create a life based on what we think we are supposed to do rather than from our own heart's desire, we always feel like something is missing, that we are not quite free. There is a deeper longing that keeps calling us to stop conforming, to break the chains of our fears, to jump the fence of people's opinions and find our innate wild happiness.

Inside, your essence whispers to you to remember your light. The authentic feminine waits to be embodied in your form.

Your being yearns to blossom, to share your soul's love. You taste it, you sense it. When you attune to your inner bounty, life is glorious. Each breath is a joy. The external form does not matter. You know your own wholeness, and you feel complete when you are alone or with others.

By aligning with Warrior Goddess wisdom, you have given yourself a big gift of choosing a pathway that will encourage you to face and clear out the old power structures and reclaim your authenticity. You are not trying to take on the image of being someone you are not; instead, you allow your inner truth and beauty to be free from the weight of your fears and outdated beliefs. As you accept and honor yourself, you suddenly stop needing to be different, and you see the unique, perfect creation that you are. All of you is magnificent, even the parts you wish were different.

It's time to be honest about what your definition of power has been, and then let it go completely in favor of embodying *your* power. Let go of all your expectations about what your path will look like, or who you will become. You don't know! It is a mystery! You step into true divine Warrior Goddess energy when you no longer need to define yourself as this or that.

Stepping into a new power means doing the work and having the courage to unweave the tangled web of limitations, agreements, and judgments within to allow your true radiance to shine forth, and to love yourself fully along the way.

Lesson One Resources

Gifts

- What you commit to, especially your unconscious commitments, rules your actions and determines the quality and vibrancy of your life. You may have deep-seated commitments to the old power structure that no longer serve you. It's time to become aware of those and release them.

- Committing to yourself is a process that happens in layers. Committing to yourself means saying yes to all of you—both the parts you love and the parts you dislike.

- Power does not come from who you know, what you do, or how much money you have in the bank. It comes from blossoming into unconditional love for yourself and embodying joyful faith in your gifts.

- When you let go of who you wish you were, you reclaim your power to be radiantly, magnetically, and creatively who you are.

Explorations

Moving from Old to New

Where are you still hooked to old reflections of power? How are your judgments and fears tied to an old power matrix? Write down your answers to these questions over the next few weeks.

One great way to purge yourself of old ways of power is to name them without making yourself or others wrong. Here are some other questions to help you explore this idea further:

- Do you find your self-worth in how you look, or is your self-worth an inner spring based in your self-acceptance and respect?

- Do you base your value on how well you are taking care of everyone else at the expense of yourself, or do you honor the importance of self-care and loving boundaries?

- Does your strength come from how much money you have, how sexy you are, or who you know, or does it flow from your inner peace and resilience?

Keep questioning and writing down what true power means to you, and pay attention, without judgment, for where you give your power away.

Female Role Models

Who are your role models? Who do you strive to be like? Our role models can be teachers, family members, fictional characters in movies or on TV, public women or private women. Role models and mentors are very important to inspire us and give us courage to take risks. Honor these women who inspire you for their contribution and wisdom, but recognize that you are not going to be just like them; do not use them against yourself. Be aware of the sneakiness of self-judgment. Surrender to your own unfolding, in your own time. Let go of using other women's accomplishments and grace to beat yourself up; instead be inspired and motivated by the beauty and skill around you. As you name the women who inspire you, write down the qualities and actions of what Warrior Goddess power they embody, such as presence, courage, passion, honesty, compassion, and clarity. In the next Warrior Goddess lesson you will take your new commitment to self and create a new foundation by learning how to align with, rather than being in fear of or trying to control, life.

Align with Life

I love to see a young girl go out and grab the world by the lapels. Life's a bitch. You've got to go out and kick ass.

—Maya Angelou

For most of my childhood, one of my favorite sayings was "It's not fair!"

It wasn't fair that we moved all the time (eight times while I was growing up, to four different countries). It wasn't fair that in the sixth grade my sister got a new bike before I did (and, to heap on the injustice, she was younger than I was). It wasn't fair that I didn't make the cheerleading squad on my first try, or that I was shorter than everyone in my class.

As an adult, I continued to believe life should go the way I wanted it to go. When it did, I was happy. When it didn't, I was miserable. Without realizing it, I had adopted a model of conditional happiness.

I carried this "it isn't fair" attitude with me into college, politics, and relationships, where it started morphing into a new belief: "If I just did things right, everything would go as it was supposed to." (I mean, that sounds fair, doesn't it?) When

I couldn't control the external world, I tried to make things better by transferring the sense of "Life isn't right when . . ." to "I'm not right unless . . ." Then all I had to do was fix myself. The problem was that what I considered to be "right" was an illusionary image of perfection that changed depending on what I thought people around me wanted me to be.

As you can imagine, this created all sorts of suffering. I brought the belief "I'm not right unless . . ." to everything I did, trying to follow the rules so I could be accepted and loved.

In college when I was immersed in politics and fighting for justice, there was one set of unspoken rules for how I needed to look and act to be "right": Wear long skirts and a T-shirt with slogans. No bra. Have long hair. Judge and condemn anyone not on our side. Be angry and rail against the establishment.

Later, I embraced spirituality, and there was a different set of unspoken rules: Love everyone. Wear loose, flowing clothing and lots of sacred jewelry. Have faith. Always be kind and generous and selfless. Help others.

When we try to be who we believe we are supposed to be, or try to always follow the rules—spoken and unspoken agreements—without awareness, our actions are aligned with fear. No matter how fabulous the organization, community, religion, spirituality, family, relationship, or business, we bring our fear of not being accepted, of being abandoned, of needing to do it "right."

The result is trying to contort ourselves to fit an image. The message we tell ourselves remains the same: You are not right the way you are. We align with who we think we should be, rather than with who we are.

And this focus on how we should be on the outside basically makes us crazy, unhappy, and confused on the inside.

During my apprenticeship with don Miguel Ruiz, the author of *The Four Agreements*, I became immersed in the Toltec teachings of his family. The Toltec teachings show us a pathway to freedom by encouraging us to question all our agreements so we can shift from being judgmental jailers of our spirit to artists of our spirit.

As Allan Hardman writes in *The Everything Toltec Wisdom Book* (pronouns changed to the feminine):

As an artist of the spirit, the Toltec of today knows there are no rules she must follow, no belief system she is required to embrace, and no leaders to obey. She seeks complete freedom from fear, and absolute surrender to love and acceptance. The modern Toltec discovers a happiness that is the result of love and acceptance flowing out of her, and she knows there is an endless supply of love—it is her nature to love. She embraces life, and dances in joy and gratitude for every moment of her existence. This is the Toltec path and this is the modern spiritual warrior—an artist of the spirit.

The truth is simple: Life is perfectly imperfect, unpredictable, and unexplainable. A Warrior Goddess does not try to control life or even understand it. Our job is to consciously choose what we are aligning with and then let go, and dance in joy and gratitude for every moment of existence.

The choice comes down to fear versus love. Do you want to be a punitive judge or flattened victim toward life, or a Warrior Goddess artist, delighting in the many diverse colors and shapes of creation? Do you want to struggle with what should be, or show up to flow with what is in this moment? When we honor the cycles of life we learn to love and learn from all the textures, from the rough edges to the silky smooth synchronicities.

As Warrior Goddesses, we are all works in progress. While I am not always able to have faith when things are difficult, when I do my life flows with grace and joy and ease. And I've learned that when I am in struggle, like I was over the end of my marriage, being kind and gentle to myself as I practice letting go creates more space for surrender than fierce judgment.

Change is natural. As we honor the flows of life—birth and death, coming together and splitting apart—and look for the beauty in both the flourishing, bright flower *and* in the fading, browning bloom, we find balance and acceptance.

Cyclical Living

Life flows within and around us, connecting us with all of nature. Life is the creative force of the Divine; its source is unlimited potential. So within the form of all things, from a rock to a flower to our bones, dwells pure potential, undivided from source.

We always have access to this spirit grace, as we are part of the life-force and are therefore irrevocably connected to God/ Goddess/Earth/Sky. But our attention is mostly hooked by our day-to-day existence and our attachments, or our strong preferences for certain outcomes. Often we miss the immensity of our being by focusing on the details and dramas around us. We stay in the crust of life and forget the depth of connection we are capable of.

Life flows, swiftly bringing change and growth.

When we align with life, we choose to align with *all* of life, not just the parts we like or are comfortable with—and not just when everything goes our way. Aligning with life means truly knowing and accepting that aging, death, sickness, natural disasters, accidents, humans and their wacky ways—all these things are bound to alter our course. Aligning with life means understanding that you cannot control the cycles of nature.

We cause our own suffering, not because life is so big and unpredictable, but because we are attached to our desires and expectations. Cyclical living teaches us to embrace the ups and downs of life. Through tapping the truth we learn to go beneath our own preferences and dreams to understand the natural cycles of the rising and falling away of all things. We learn to take nothing personally, especially not the force of life.

This is quite a dance! As we come more and more into our center we learn to find the balance of personal will and sacred surrender. We begin to know what it is we want, and put our energy 100 percent behind our will. And at the same time we must surrender to the truth that the Universe is much, much bigger than we are! If we try to demand that our needs get met, or feel victimized if we do not get our way, we fall back into on old dream that we can control everything around us.

The idea that we can control the people and things around us is an illusion. Occasionally when we force our will onto a situation we get our desired outcome, so we buy into the false belief that we have control. But truly, the only way to be authentically centered is to see the ebb and flow of life not from your personal wants, but from the point of view of life itself. Life does not personally punish people or seek to cause suffering; it simply moves. It is only when we claim life should look this way or that way that we limit ourselves and suffer. From the big point of view, the death of a child or the devastation of a hurricane is as much a part of life as the beauty of a sunset or falling in love.

This lesson is much easier to think about than to embody, as it means radically shifting our perception of the world and our place in it. It means moving beyond the victim-judge dual-ity, the voices of, "Oh, I have no power, there is no hope and no point in life," or "I can create anything I want to and never feel any yucky emotions or unpleasant experiences." Between these two places is a point of humility and grace and great faith.

To align with life in this way, Warrior Goddesses start by following the wisdom of our ancestors and shifting from modern-day "linear living" back to a more natural and calm "cyclical living."

Living within the Cycles

Linear living is goal-oriented and filled with expectations. We live linearly when we believe that if we do A and then B and then C we will arrive at D. Or, when we expect something to already be done. Impatience, judgment, stress, and frustration can be the result of too much linear living and thinking.

While there are plenty of places that linear thinking is invalu-able (such as balancing your checkbook, following a specific recipe, or organizing a large business project), living life as if it were predictably linear is a huge hindrance to creativity, joy, and sanity.

As a young adult, I rebelled against both linear and cycli-cal thought. I just wanted what I wanted when I wanted it. I didn't want to follow logical steps, or be patient and honor the cycles. But life has a way of showing us that following the "right" steps does not guarantee an outcome. I think of my friend Laura, who married her beloved, finished her engineer-ing degree, and had a great job. When her husband got sick with cancer, she systematically went through every possible cure, from doctors to herbs, believing she could find the solution if she just followed the right steps. When he died it took years for her to come to understand that life is a cycle, and that her trying to control the outcome created so much more suffering than his death.

Now I love both linear and cyclical thinking. I've learned that linear thinking is best held as a tool within the flow of life's natural cycles, rather than a lifestyle. When we try to force life into a logical, linear framework, we suffer. When we open to the wisdom of cyclical ebb and flow, like our ancestors did, we thrive.

In ancient times, individuals and communities shared in the cyclical changes of nature by gathering to celebrate the equinoxes and solstices. Every part of the cycle, from recent deaths to new births, was honored. Coming together in community gave all the people a pause from their day-to-day life to witness the cycles of change in their community, and a marker to notice what had changed for them internally since the last gathering. This allowed them to feel like they were a part of the whole, and to choose where they wanted to put their energy in the coming months.

In modern times, you might feel a sense of separation from the cyclical nature of change. Electric lights, fixed work hours, and linear thinking all distance you from the natural ebb and flow of the natural world. And now that we can communicate instantaneously via e-mail and text messages you might believe that internal transformation or external change should happen this instant. The result of this kind of mental pressure is frustration, self-judgment, and confusion.

The life cycle of a plant is a great metaphor for all cycles. When we plant a seed in the ground, we push it into the darkness of earth. A miraculous, hidden process happens that takes that hard seed and cracks it open to let the life out. If we impatiently keep digging up the seed to see if it is sprouting, we risk stopping the process of growth.

Once the first vibrant green tendril pushes up through the soil, our little plant needs nourishment: sun and water and care. Too much or not enough sun or water can kill our tiny sprout, so we must stay connected to it and listen to what its needs are. As it grows its needs change.

There is a time when the plant may lose its leaves and go dormant, or reach the end of its life cycle. Its energy goes back into the soil, creating nourishment for the next thing to grow.

When we start a new project, relationship, or spiritual practice we are planting a seed. There is a certain amount of faith in starting something new, a leap into the mystery.

Sometimes that new seed of change germinates, sometimes it doesn't. To give any new idea, relationship, or intent the best chance for growth, we need to listen to its needs and consciously nourish it with our attention, presence, and care—just like a tender plant. We are learning along the way. And everything has a life cycle. When something falls apart or dies, we honor the cycle of letting go and grieving until we can look back in gratitude. We can then explore what tweaks we might want to make for the next cycle.

Remember, you cannot control life. It unfolds in unexpected ways. As a Warrior Goddess you know that while life doesn't always go the way you would like it to, your power comes not from how strongly you can resist what you don't like, but in how calmly and serenely you align yourself with life's challenges. And a big part of this is learning to balance intent and surrender. This means knowing when to take action for something you believe in or want, and knowing when to let go and trust the flow.

In recognizing and aligning with the cycles rather than fighting them, a Warrior Goddess understands that going with the flow of life is not a sign of weakness, but rather strength. There are gifts to be received in every one of the "low points" in these cycles if we are willing and able to see them.

Aligning with Manifestation

When we align with life, we learn a beautiful Toltec Warrior Goddess art: Balancing being 100 percent clear with what we want (our intent), and being 100 percent at peace with the outcome of the situation.

Say you want a new car. You want a red car, specifically that beautiful Prius your neighbor has. You dream about it, set your intent, wish, hope. The truth is that you do not have enough resources to own a car, but you put 100 percent of your energy behind your desire for this new car.

In the meantime the Universe sends you many gifts: a sweet red bike, a used car, a carpool opportunity. You ignore all of them, because you are fixated and attached to the Prius. The truth is that if you really stop and look at what your true needs are—safe transportation, decent gas mileage, a low carbon footprint—you will quickly see that the Universe has provided as much. But what your ego wants is to feel rich and sexy in a brand-new red Prius.

So often life flows and brings us gifts, true gifts that will nourish our highest intent, but we miss them because we are focusing on comfort or an old dream or a picture we have of how things are supposed to be. To align with life, you must first get clear about what you actually want on a feeling level. So from the example above, let's say you feel into what you really want and you recognize it is reliable transportation that is safe and affordable. Then when the red bike shows up on your doorstep you will recognize it for what it is: "Ah, this is the manifestation of my desire for a red car, which is really my desire for transportation! And how cool, it will also help me in my desire to get in shape!" This is aligning with life.

Sometimes what you want to manifest is internal, such as "I want more peace in my life" or "I want to love myself." The same principles apply whether you want to manifest a new job or self-love. Get clear on your intent. Open to how it will manifest. Pay attention.

The paradox is to know what you want, put your energy behind it 100 percent, and then let your intention go to a higher force. Work from your feeling sense rather than from your mind. Stay open and curious about what shows up. Sometimes what shows up is the obstacle that needs to be cleared from your being before you will be able to open fully to your highest possibility. The path of the Warrior Goddess teaches you to practice unraveling the obstacle without suffering over it or using it against yourself.

So how do you know if you are aligning with life or forcing the flow? If the thing you are putting your focus toward does not manifest immediately, or it does manifest but not how you wanted it, or it simply doesn't manifest at all, do you suffer? If not getting what you wanted causes you to suffer, then you know that you are attached to the outcome. You are not aligning with life fully, but with your attachment to how things are supposed to look. If there is no suffering but a renewed sense of "Yes! Let's try again," then you are aligned with life.

There is space for unexpected outcomes and the joy that comes from going after what you want, regardless of whether it arrives as you expected. You may have grief or sorrow or anger, but there is no story attached to it, only an emotion that moves through you, leaving you feeling clearer and more open (and perhaps a bit exhausted from releasing).

From the mindset of a victim, the energy would look like this: "This isn't fair! Why is this happening to me? Why is God deserting me? I am all alone; I am helpless. I am guilty. It is my fault. This is my parents' fault. This is not OK." From the mindset of resistance and judgment, our response would look like this: "This is a horrible situation created by horrible people. They must be punished! It is their fault! I must avenge this situation, and I will use my anger to do so!"

In either case, we stop listening to the flow of life and fixate on our internal voices. These voices come not from our highest source within, but from our egos and adherence to outdated beliefs. And whenever we allow these things to control us, we are living from unconscious agreements that are rooted in the past, rather than the beauty and peace that exists in the present moment.

One of our Warrior Goddess sisters in Austin recently wrote me to apologize for not being in class. Her rheumatoid arthritis was causing her a lot of pain, so she needed to be quiet and rest her body. She later e-mailed me this question: "I am trying hard not to judge myself and learn to accept my body how it is now. Not an easy task on some days. How do I accept what I don't want?"

It is not an easy task to accept what we don't want—especially when what we are experiencing is pain or suffering. I wrote her back with compassion and invited her to be with what was true for her body right now, without making up any story about what it would be like tomorrow. Acceptance is not a dispirited surrender from a place of powerlessness; acceptance and aligning with life is an active, courageous walk with the flow of what is. When we tell ourselves the truth of this moment ("Right now my body needs to rest"), then we can stay present and listen to how to best nourish this body, situation, and time in our lives. When we love the limitations, we find all sorts of creative ways to love ourselves.

The transition from aligning with our preferences and ego to aligning with life is a big leap, and it takes a lot of time, practice, and faith. But the reward is immense. Be patient with yourself and do this work bit by bit. Keep asking yourself, "What do I really want?" Go beyond the initial desire to the depth of your yearning. Now, how can you give this quality to yourself?

So often we look outside ourselves for something to fulfill us. We best align with life when we learn to open and bring the energy we are looking for into our own being. From this place of fullness your vision will clear, the golden thread of Spirit will guide you, and you will tap into the infinite potential in each moment.

Lesson Two Resources

Gifts

- Life is neither fair nor unfair. Life is a force that constantly moves and changes.

- Shifting from linear or circular living relieves stress and returns us to our natural harmony and balance.

- Aligning with life means committing to our intent, or goals, 100 percent *as well as* surrendering to the outcome, whatever it may be.

- While we cannot control life, we do have a choice in how we respond to what life brings and how we react.

Explorations

Clear Alignment

What do you really want? Sometimes it is hard to know. Start being proactive in getting to clarity by asking yourself, "What do I want now?" regularly throughout your day. Then connect this clarity with awareness of what is happening now and what is possible. Here's an example: I get quiet and listen to my body, and I feel that I want Thai food for lunch instead of the hamburger that someone offered to pick up for me (clarity). But I'm on deadline and do not have the time to get Thai food (reality). So I ask again, "What do I want?" and I realize that I want something light. So I opt for the salad bar at the deli next door.

This simple example can be expanded to much more complex things. The formula is the same. Ask yourself what you want. Look at what is actually true and present in the moment. Ask yourself again what you want. See what you can align to in this moment.

Surrendering the Little Things

Practice, practice, practice! That is what it takes to learn to surrender and let go. So use every opportunity you have to let things go in a graceful way. Start small. Is there anything in your house that you really don't like? Donate it to a thrift store or give it to a friend. Give away the clothes that don't fit you. If something in your life doesn't work out, practice shaking it off and looking at what is working. Where else can you practice surrendering? Notice all the little places in your life to open your hands and let go. This will help with the bigger life surrenders, like the end of relationships, or aging, or changes at work.

Imagine that you are holding hands with the first two Warrior Goddess lessons. On your left is your commitment to yourself; on your right is your alignment with life. Say yes to these two new allies, and invite them to be your new ears and your new eyes. Hold their hands with love, and let them guide you in all your actions.

In the next lesson you will invite in the third point to your new stabilizing foundation: purifying your vessel. You will learn how to make the vital transformational shift from seeing yourself as not good enough to deeply honoring and respecting yourself. We'll practice joyfully clearing out obstacles and anything that does not serve you so that you can let your natural radiance shine. Let's go, Warrior Goddess!

Purify Your Vessel

The thing that is really hard, and really amazing, is giving up on being perfect and beginning the work of becoming yourself.

—Anna Quindlen

In becoming a Warrior Goddess, our first two lessons focused on committing to ourselves and aligning with life. For these two things to work effectively, we must purify what I call our "vessel." This vessel is defined as a sacred container of awareness that holds all of you. Your mind, energy, emotions, and physical body are all part of the vehicle for the spirit, or the invisible essence that is at your core. Your vessel houses your spirit, and your spirit cannot express fully if your vessel is burdened by things that don't serve you.

Specifically, this means we must become aware of and consciously clear out all the beliefs, stories, fears, and general gunk that is clogging our system. And this takes rolling up our warrior sleeves and getting to work while we also open to divine goddess grace and inspiration.

Our first step in purifying all aspects of self is to learn to be in a relationship with ourselves in a new way by creating our vessel—an imaginary container that keeps us inner-focused and prevents us from becoming hooked into the multitude of opinions and stories that are constantly competing for our attention throughout the day. These could include messages from the media, opinions of friends, expectations of relatives—all of which can trigger the familiar sabotaging voice of self-judgment and self-doubt.

When you create a strong container of self-awareness around yourself, you stop leaking your inner-power through self-criticism, judgment, comparison, and doubt. This container of your presence and self-acceptance needs to be strong to allow the fires of transformation to burn away all that doesn't serve you.

Creating a Container

Imagine a container that holds you tenderly and securely. This container lovingly embraces you and clearly defines the boundary of what is yours and what belongs to others.

By creating a container that embraces you during change, you hold the space necessary to move through any upheaval, turmoil, or fear generated by your internal alchemy. The heat of transformation, the quickening of forces shifting from one state to another, brings a great deal of energy, and for many, it can cause some discomfort. An appropriate container surrounds all of you—comfortable, uncomfortable, and everything in between. It forms a stable scaffolding that remains firm while you destabilize and dissolve what no longer works for you.

The strength of this vital personal container is imbued with energy from the goddess of compassion and balanced with the energy of fierce warrior commitment. As you build this container of unconditional acceptance, you will be able to hold yourself through the uncomfortable passages. Learn to love the complete cycle of your process of transformation, which will have a beginning, a middle, and an end. During the journey, you will be challenged, shaken, scared, exuberant, and confident, sometimes all at the same time! Can you become larger than the part of you that guards the status quo, wiser than the myriad of strategies you use to keep yourself limited, and more expanded than your need for safety?

Yes! You can learn to hold yourself. Yes! You can learn to trust your judgment and intuitions. Yes! You can learn to nourish yourself. It requires transforming old beliefs and patterns of being.

To build a steady container, you must be willing to:

- Stop defining yourself by what you do or who you know.

- Embrace all aspects of yourself; honor your strengths and acknowledge your weaknesses.

- Know your truth in this moment, and hold to your truth even in the face of adversity.

- Consciously choose your friends and support system.

- Let go of the need for people to like you.

- Soothe yourself when you are upset or scared.

- Put yourself out there; pursue your highest purpose.

- Become your own best friend and ally.

- Clear out buried emotions.

- Stay present with yourself under stress.

- Claim loving acceptance of your physical body.

- Be mindful of what substances you put into your body.

To cast a circle is to create sacred space between the spiritual and the physical realms. By stepping into Warrior Goddess Training you are energetically joining together with other Warrior Goddess women to form a structure that will support you mentally, emotionally, spiritually, and physically in firmly linking with the truest expression of your inner knowing. This in-between place is where the alchemy of transformation happens. It will be sweet and scary, blissful and terrifying, easy and challenging beyond anything you can imagine.

Sacred Full-Being Cleaning

From the witness of your Warrior Goddess container of love and presence, you can now begin to purify your mind and untangle its influence on your energy, emotions, and body. The first step to purifying these four inner aspects of yourself is knowing where you are at this moment. Become aware of your current state of mind, your energy level, your emotions, and your body by answering the following questions:

- Notice the chatter that fills your mind. What are the themes that you hear most?

- How often do you have stretches of silence and mental quiet?

- How clogged or free-flowing is your energetic being? Do you feel energetically bright or dim? How stagnant or volatile is your emotional body? Do you overreact to situations? (Remember, a reaction can be internal or external.)

- How much fluidity and openness do you have emotionally? Are you able to release emotions cleanly and move on?

- Do you love and respect your physical body, or do you mentally judge your physical form?

- How do you feel about your weight? Are you accepting of your body, or are you unsatisfied?

- Do you feel at peace or judgmental about your age or appearance?

Look at the chart below, and taking each section one at a time, read the words in the left-hand column.

Overview of Self—Current	
MENTAL	**Percent Right Now**
Clarity/Peace	
Chatter/Confusion	
ENERGETIC	
Brightness/Fullness	
Dimness/Contraction	
EMOTIONAL	
Fluidity/Openness	
Stagnation/Being triggered	
PHYSICAL	
Acceptance/Love	
Rejection/Judgment	

Notice how you feel internally as you read the two sets of words. Take a breath. Close your eyes and invite yourself to explore what you experience as you move from one polarity to the other.

Now do a quick survey, without thinking. Look at the aspects in the left-hand column (mental, energetic, emotional, physical), and then at the two polarities. Write a percentage for each one so that together they total 100 percent. For example, you might feel you have 40 percent mental clarity and 60 percent mental chatter at this time in your life. Don't think! Just write the percentages that come to you.

This will give you a sense of where you still need to do some scrubbing and polishing!

Before you go any further, stop and take a breath. Look at the percentages you wrote in the chart and notice how you feel as you look at your numbers. If you have any self-judgment or frustration or sense of exhaustion or confusion, take a moment to adjust your attitude. Yes, you may have a lot of work to do. Yes, you may be really out of whack in one or all of the areas of your being. Yes, you may feel you are not moving fast enough. So try this: Do the exercise again, but this time from the perspective of where you were five (or more) years ago. Start by closing your eyes and putting yourself into the past, and then do the percentages without thinking.

Overview of Self—Five Years Ago	
MENTAL	**Percent Five Years Ago**
Clarity/Peace	
Chatter/Confusion	
ENERGETIC	
Brightness/Fullness	
Dimness/Contraction	
EMOTIONAL	
Fluidity/Openness	
Stagnation/Being triggered	
PHYSICAL	
Acceptance/Love	
Rejection/Judgment	

This second chart will hopefully help you see that you have shifted a lot over the past five years. And you may notice some areas that are more enduring. All can be changed over time with guidance, action, and perseverance. What will hasten the transformation is becoming aware of your inner judge and victim and learning to witness rather than believe their voices.

The Inner Judge and Victim

Within our mind all of us carry the seeds of self-sabotage in the form of two negative voices. One voice is the judge, and one is the victim. These two voices are siblings of the same parents, which are fear and self-rejection.

Your inner judge, or critic, is constantly looking for what you or others are not doing right. Your judge doesn't just have high standards; it has impossible standards. Nothing you do is right. Sometimes the judge keeps its focus on what it perceives to be your fatal flaws, sometimes it turns its eye to those around you. Either way, when you listen to the judge's voice as a source of wisdom, you are caught in comparison and frustration.

Your victim, or the I-can't-do-it-I'm-not-enough part of you, is always looking to a judge for validation, which it never gets. The victim will always seek out a judge, whether internal or external, to prove its unworthiness. When you listen to the victim's voice as the truth, you spend your days feeling powerless and without hope.

How can you joyfully clear your divine goddess being when the judge is so often your eyes and ears? How can you take clear warrior action when your victim whines in the corner? Here is the awesome Warrior Goddess attitude adjustment: Go from viewing yourself as a broken, misused, misunderstood, not loveable, not good enough woman to feeling yourself as a magnificent temple, a vessel of the divine feminine that needs a thorough, sacred remodeling from the inside out. Remember that it is your judge that tracks the most mud into your sacred temple! Note: There is a difference between judgment and discernment. When we judge others or ourselves, we create more messes; when we are discerning, there is no emotional or energetic charge in our being—it is simply a choice. The difference is in the energy. If there is blame or rejection, this is judgment. If there is compassion and clarity, this is discernment. Let's say I'd like to lose a few pounds that I gained over the winter. A judgment of self would sound like this: "I am fat. I hate my body. I wish things were different." Discernment would sound more like this: "I feel sluggish and would like to lose ten pounds and get in better shape. I think my body would feel better if I did so."

Let's next look at an example of judgment and discernment in regards to others. I have a family member who borrowed some money and never paid it back. Here's a judging statement: "This dishonest, lazy person should get a job and pay her bills! What is wrong with her? Doesn't she have any honor?" Here's what discernment sounds like: "This person obviously has some financial issues that she needs to work through. If she asks to borrow money again, I can either loan it to her or not, but if I do so, it will be with no expectation of repayment."

In both cases, judgment leaves you feeling negative, heavy, or self-important. Discernment leaves no trace.

As you purify your vessel by no longer believing the lies of the judge and victim you will know the truth: You are precious. Your mind, energy, emotions, and body are sacred, no matter what state of disarray they may be in at the current moment. You are a holy vessel, the Holy Grail, a sacred chalice.

The sanctity of your being cannot be compromised, violated, or diminished. It can be buried under layers of fear, filled with gunk, tarnished, and bruised. But beneath all of your self-betrayal and self-abuse, you are pure. You are whole. You are the twinkle of the Goddess's eye.

Remember: there is no knight in white armor coming to save your butt. No spiritual teacher will be arriving to cleanse you of all your sins and leave you forever glowing. And your spiritual judge will not be able to shame, beat, or threaten you into enlightenment, no matter how hard it tries to make you "right." In reality, you must be your own knight, your own angel, your own spiritual guide, and your own slayer of the demon judge/victim monster.

Let's continue our Warrior Goddess heroine's journey by freeing ourselves from the judge and victim stories that weigh us down.

Purifying Exercises

As we're purifying our vessel, it helps to break things down into bite-sized pieces. Below is a guide to purifying actions. I've separated these actions into different areas: mind, energy, emotions, and physical. Start by picking one aspect to focus on. You are not trying to get to 100 percent. Keep it bite-sized!

Pick one or more of the ideas below; then set a time line for how long you will do them for. Be committed to purifying your mind for the time allotted. Imagine you are blessed with the sacred job of keeping the Warrior Goddess temple clean, remembering that *you* are the temple. Bring all of your love and devotion to cleansing what no longer serves you and creating more light and sacredness in your being.

Clear Your Mind

Your mind and thoughts have a huge effect on all aspects of your being, so it is an important place to start deep cleaning! When the mind is stuck in judgment or victim mode, it tracks all sorts of debris into our sacred temple of self. A purified mind sees the world through the eyes of the witness, with curiosity and patience. These exercises will help you find clarity and stillness in your mind.

- Meditate for five to ten minutes each day. Practice clearing your mind of clutter and focusing on your breath. Witness the busyness of your mind. When you're sitting, sometimes your mind will keep chattering the whole time; stay steady. The practice of sitting will bring more calmness into the rest of your life, even when it seems you are doing it wrong! Trust your intent to get quiet. See the books in the Further Reading section for more support.

- Make a commitment to stop judging yourself. Keep your awareness strong. Imagine the judge tracking mud into your temple, and send it outside. Know that you may do this a couple hundred times a day. Be diligent in not feeding your judge.

- Start speaking your truth and telling yourself the truth, without punishment. If you notice yourself telling a lie or partial truth, go back to the person and clean it up. It can be awkward, but it is a great practice that clears up a lot of confusion and mental shuffling. When we tell ourselves the truth about what we want or do not want in our lives, we cut out a lot of chatter. When we are willing to speak our truth to others without rejecting ourselves, our sense of integrity returns. Stop listening to the same old recording in your head; hit the erase button, and record a new positive statement to focus on.

Channel Your Energy

Have you ever sensed that someone was behind you before hearing or seeing them? Can you imagine what it would feel like to walk into a roomful of angry people, even if you were blindfolded? Do you have days when you feel drained and days when you feel like you've been recharged? We are each not only physical beings but also energetic, and we often sense or experience things in our energetic body before we are aware of them mentally or physically. Our energetic body permeates and extends beyond our physical body, and just like our body needs regular exercise, attention, and cleaning, so too does our energy. These exercises will help you learn to clear and protect your energetic body.

- Do a daily energetic cleansing ceremony with fire. Light a candle and ask the flame to help you burn away any stuck energetic patterns or any energy you've picked up that does not serve you. Breathe the fire into your being; visualize it clearing the tangled brush of old agreements and unbeneficial energies. Use your hands to trace the edge of your energetic field, which is about arm's length from your body, defining and claiming your edges. Then breathe in the vitality of the fire and fill yourself up with energy and vibrancy all the way to the edge of your field.

- Practice containing your energy. When we are not aware, our energy can be affected by other people's attitudes and opinions. If you are sensitive to other people's energetic or emotional states, you can learn to protect your energetic field. Energy follows imagination, so your best tool is your imagination. I like to imagine myself wearing a beautiful cloak that filters out harmful energy but lets loving energy pass through.

- Once a week go for a walk in nature. Call in the trees and spirits and juiciness of nature around you. When you feel full, pick a flat space and run as fast as you can for a quick burst. Stop. Feel the energy rushing through your system and feed it to every part of you. Get bigger, bigger, and bigger! Connect to nature from this bigness. Now walk slowly, calming your breath and letting all of your muscles relax completely. Get soft inside. Get quiet. Bring your energy close inside of you and ground it into the earth. Slowly come to a stop and stand still, finding your internal energetic balance. Reach out and connect to nature from this still center. Repeat three times, practicing energetic fluidity and exploring the polarities of big energy and still energy.

Check In with Your Emotional State

Have you heard the phrase "flooded with emotion"? Water is all about movement, and we're striving to release our grip on our emotions and let them flow naturally. Throughout our lifetime we're going to experience all kinds of emotions, and we want to allow ourselves to feel deeply, reflect on those feelings, and then move on. These exercises will help you heal your emotional body and move stagnant energy.

- Take five minutes each day, whether you feel like it or not, to move through some emotions. You can also do this by dancing vigorously and yelling. Use your voice; scream, cry, om, growl . . . let your emotions *move!*

- To clear old emotions: Find a movie that touches the specific emotion you are working with (grief, fear, anger, etc.). As you're watching the movie, allow yourself to go into the emotion fully, with the intent that on the other side you'll tap into your awareness to find the specific story you are telling yourself. When you finish emoting, notice if you feel lighter or heavier. If heavier, whom do you need to forgive? What do you need to release from the past? Watch yourself over the next few days to see if your mind starts to re-create the story. Shift your focus to a mantra or chant, or practice opening and breathing fully. Do not let your mind restimulate the emotion. And if the emotion does come up, go express it!

- There is a very strong, dysfunctional relationship between the mind and the emotional body that keeps emotions trapped in our body instead of allowing them to arise and clear. Practice witnessing your emotions not through the filter of the judgmental mind, but from a place of curiosity. How does an emotion make your body feel? What does it do to your energetic body? Stop thinking about whether your emotions are right or wrong, good or bad, and start perceiving them from an energy point of view. Emotions are energy in motion. When we don't attach labels to them, the "negative" emotions such as anger or grief move through much more quickly, and the "positive" ones such as joy and happiness tend to stick around longer, because we are not grasping at them and fearing they will go away. How can you express the more difficult emotions without creating more internal or external drama?

Work It Out

You cannot purify your vessel without being aware of the body-mind connection. I invite you to practice radical acceptance of your body and all its features, even the ones you think you don't like. Be aware of what you put into your body and the effects these things have on you. Everyone is different based on metabolism, age, etc. There is no "one approach fits all" solution. The following exercises will help you connect to the sacred uniqueness and needs of your body.

- Do not use other people's body size to judge yourself. Stop looking at other women's bodies, and do your best to avoid magazines and TV so you stop being inundated with images. Start viewing other women as sister Warrior Goddesses and embrace them instead of being jealous of them.

- Take down or cover all the mirrors in your house, and practice feeling your body rather than looking at it all the time. Ask your body: What do you want more of? What do you want less of? Go beneath the habits and quick fixes to listen to your body's wisdom and depth.

- Exercise and/or do a cleanse. Exercising three times a week will make you feel stronger and more in your body. Use the time you exercise to bring acceptance and gratitude to your physical form.

- Be mindful of how the foods you put into your body make you feel. Notice how eating a jelly donut first thing in the morning makes you feel, or a pizza late at night. What do you feel like when you skip a meal? Also pay attention to the effects alcohol and other substances may have on your vessel. Go slow and remove one thing from your diet that is not serving you. It could be the potato chips at lunchtime, or refined sugar, or McDonald's. Or if you choose to do a physical cleanse or make a radical change in your diet, make sure you are working with a person or group with expertise in nutrition and health.

Purifying your vessel is not a solo job, but one that is best supported by a community, friends, and good guides. When you find people who can hold unconditional love and acceptance for where you are now, while encouraging you in your goals and dreams, you will feel inspired and motivated to stretch and grow. If your current community or friendships are in the old paradigm of judging and feeling victimized by the world, reach out to find new support networks. New Thought churches, such as Unity or the Center for Spiritual Living, are wonderful communities of positive support and good places to find new friendships. Most towns have a local bookstore or monthly alternative magazine where you can find inspirational events or healing practitioners to guide you on your journey back to you. As you open to accepting support in the form of friendships, or when you choose to give yourself the gift of finding a therapist, healer, or teacher, the right people will begin to appear. There are also many online communities now available, including global (and some local) Warrior Goddess Training circles. See the resources section at the end of this book for details.

Even with the best support, you are the one who will take the actions to reclaim yourself as temple, to purify your vessel. You are not alone, and you must do the work for yourself. You can do it! Cultivate this attitude, over and over again. Then when things get hard, you will draw on a clear, positive voice rather than on those unhelpful judge/victim voices that say they are helping, when in reality they are only creating more dirt and dust.

The purifying actions above are just suggestions to get your Warrior Goddess creativity mojo working. Please don't think you can't continue on your Warrior Goddess Training until you do all the tasks above, or any of the other suggestions in this book. Keep reading, keep exploring, keep taking baby steps. It's about taking action, not taking the "perfect" action.

Purifying your mind, energy, emotions, and physical self is not a one-time, check-it-off-the-list task, but a lifetime attitude shift. The truth is that life is messy. When you commit to yourself and choose to align with life, you accept the task of inner cleaning not as an icky, distasteful chore, but as a Warrior Goddess act of self-love.

Lesson Three Resources

Gifts

- To create change you must first accept where you are, and create a container of compassion and self-love that surrounds your old patterns and beliefs.

- You are a temple. When you bring the energy of honor, respect, and love to the cleaning of your temple, clearing out the old to make room for the new becomes a joy rather than a punishment.

- You are whole, beautiful, and powerful. Stop telling yourself you are broken or unredeemable.

- Create bite-sized actions to purify your vessel mentally, energetically, emotionally, and physically. What small step can you take that will create more sacred space in your being?

Explorations

Daily Purification

Just like you brush your teeth and wash your hands every day, it is important to keep your inner self clean and sparkling. Start each morning and end each day with this simple practice. Visualize a flame in your belly. Then imagine that you can take all worries, fears, caretaking thoughts, aches, and pains and offer them to the fire. Visualize the fire transmuting these energies into pure white light. Then imagine blessing yourself with the fire by breathing the white light from your feet to the top of your head.

Cleaning False Core Beliefs

Sometimes bigger issues pop up that are deeper, long-term cleaning issues. I highly recommend starting a journal so you can track what false core beliefs arise, such as "I am not love-able" or "I never do anything right." Give each false core belief a page with the belief as the title at the top. Then write a paragraph of how this false core belief manifests in your life and how it makes you feel.

Now comes the fun part: cleaning up the lies that spread from false core beliefs like muddy footprints on a clean floor. Start brainstorming examples of how your false core belief is *not* true, and write each one down. Anytime you remember or experience a truth that is opposite of your false core belief, you wipe a part of that false belief clean. As you start to name the opposites and break the pattern of believing your false core belief, you will also see what cleaning action will help you dissolve the dirt even more.

Ground Your Being and Free Your Past

> *No one can make you feel inferior*
> *without your consent.*
>
> —Eleanor Roosevelt

I once lived in a house where light bulbs would explode, electrical appliances and hard drives burnt out unexpectedly, and wall outlets would sometimes start smoking and burning. It took two electricians to fix the seemingly random calamities, and then we discovered that the problem was the entire electrical system in the house was not grounded.

Electricity flows smoothly only when it is connected to the earth. Every home has a rod that "grounds" the electrical circuits. Without this ground things go catawampus, like in my ungrounded, light bulb–exploding house.

Like many other ancient traditions (now backed by recent discoveries in quantum physics), the Toltec understood that we humans are energetic beings first and physical beings second. And as modern humans one of the places we are most out of balance energetically is around our lack of proper grounding.

When we are grounded into something solid, our energy runs smoothly. When we are ungrounded, we experience surges and crashes of energy, burnout, and dramatic explosions.

So how do we get grounded?

Let's look to nature for a new model of being.

On an energetic level, humans are a lot like trees. A well-balanced tree has deep, grounded roots that go into the earth like a grounding rod. A tree's roots are both its stability and its source of nutrition. The deeper and wider the roots, the more resilient and anchored the tree will be, and the more likely it is to survive changes in the environment, such as high winds or drought.

For example, when Hurricane Katrina hit the Gulf Coast in one of the worst natural disasters in US history, 150-year-old homes along the shoreline of Biloxi, Mississippi, were picked up by the waves and swept inland several miles. When the storm was over, the only thing left standing along the shoreline were the cypress trees, which were so grounded that even the 120-mile-per-hour winds couldn't topple them.

A well-balanced Warrior Goddess also grows deep energetic roots that sink into the earth like a grounding rod. When we are grounded in this way, we have faith in our ability to survive in the world. We trust ourselves. We feel safe and held. We are resilient.

Most women believe in order to be safe we have to send our roots and our sense of value into impermanent things: our partner, our children, our youth, our job. We define ourselves and find a sense of being worthwhile by our connection to others. While I do believe that community and connection to others is a natural flow for most women, many of us are extremely out of balance, because we don't have a central tap root that connects us to a healthy, grounded self. Our entire self-definition gets wrapped in roles like mother, wife, businesswoman, healer, or daughter, rather than our Warrior Goddess divine female essence.

Take a moment to feel where you have rooted into others to create your sense of self, safety, or belonging.

What is your main taproot? Make it deep and solid. Redirect it if it has grown attached to a person or ideal. Anchor yourself in infinity, in earth, to the life-force. Where is your true source of energy and stability? Reach deep.

Do not anchor to the specifics that will change, but to the permanent places like your own self-love, and to your own connection to the Divine. When you anchor your roots to something outside of you, you will never feel completely stable. Your beloved, kids, pets, house, parents, work, and friendships will all shift and change, no matter how stable they may appear to be. What can you anchor to that will bring true stability?

To come into a rooted Warrior Goddess sense of inner faith and security, most of us need to do some energetic housecleaning. One of the most potent places to start is by releasing old stories.

Releasing Your Old Stories

As women, we are filled to the brim with stories, woven by learned beliefs and agreements of what it means to be a female, that keep us tied to past old beliefs and keep us from our true potential. Do you ever feel that you are weighted down by your past and buried under layers of self-doubt, fears, and confusion?

When I first started apprenticing with don Miguel Ruiz and working with the Toltec teachings, I felt like a suitcase that was overstuffed with all the ideas of who I thought I should be. My entire inside world was crowded and heavy. I knew I wanted to lighten my load. But at first I didn't know how to change, I just knew I wanted to. As I learned to hold myself in a container of compassionate awareness and refrain from judging, I began to notice the impact my words had on my relationship to myself.

One day, as I was sharing the story of my life with a new friend, I had an epiphany. I realized that my story was not a factual collection of words describing my life. My story was a heavy anchor I was dragging behind me while trying to catch the wind in my sails.

My story used to go like this: I was traumatized as a child by how often my family moved. I went to eight different schools and lived in four countries—Singapore, Hong Kong, the United States, and Thailand—by the time I was sixteen. We would move every two years or so. I started off at each school feeling painfully shy, disconnected, and alone. By the second year I would have made friends and found my groove, and then we would move again and the cycle would start over. Because of the many times I moved away from friends, or they moved away because of their parents' jobs, I have a hard time connecting with people intimately and I'm afraid of being abandoned.

Each time I told my story I felt sorry for myself. Wouldn't you?

And on that day with my new friend I had the awareness to lovingly release my past frame of perception and rewrite my history as an adventure rather than a disaster. This was my new story: I was blessed as a child with an adventurous family. We moved every two years and traveled around the world every summer. I spent most of my childhood going to great international schools in Southeast Asia, and by the time I was sixteen my family had visited or lived in twenty different countries, including Thailand, Singapore, India, Egypt, Italy, and Spain. Because of the many times we moved and traveled I learned to be incredibly flexible and to deeply love the diversity and creativity of humans. My childhood experiences helped me relate to many different perspectives, to make friends easily, and to celebrate change.

Each time I told this new story, I felt a sense of adventure and lots of gratitude. How does it make you feel?

Now the important question: Which story is true?

Both stories are true and not true, depending on my perspective. The answer isn't about which one is the absolute truth, but which story feels most in alignment with who I am and who I want to be. One is a story of a victim of life; the second is a claimed story of a Warrior Goddess.

The Warrior Goddess path takes awareness and merges it with action to create inner change. Awareness shows us where we are stuck in a heavy past; transformation brings us into the lightness of a consciously chosen present.

Choosing to be a Warrior Goddess woman means looking at ourselves as a palette of colors and textures, and noticing which colors and textures nourish and enliven us, and which drain or dull us. It is only when we become aware that a certain story, action, or behavior doesn't feed us that we can change it.

Today my internal world has much more space, and what is unnecessary baggage is much more obvious. I now see internal unpacking as a sweet ongoing process of inner cleaning, like washing the dishes or brushing my teeth.

Transformation starts with how we use our words—how we speak our story to ourselves and others. Like body and mind, words are vessels. Each word we choose can hold the vibration of healing, peace, and love, or be brimming with fear, victimization, and judgment. Our words help to nourish or deplete our vessel.

Even the same sentence can increase or decrease our enthusiasm, depending on the energy behind the words. I can say to someone, "You are doing great!" and infuse these four words with enthusiasm and support. Or I can say, "You are doing great" with sarcasm and bitterness and the message is conveyed very differently, even if the words seem positive.

Awareness leads to understanding and clarity of what is working and what is not working. Clarity leads to taking personal responsibility to transform our old patterns and habits. Responsibility leads to releasing blame, guilt, and shame. And when we release blame, guilt, and shame, we are free to choose, with gratitude, which story we want to believe.

Exercise: Releasing Your Old Stories

Now it is time to put our Warrior Goddess theory into action! Take some time right now to rewrite a story you have been telling yourself that is weighing you down.

Think about one or two main stories you have told yourself about past events that cause you suffering. Most of us don't have to dig too deep for these, as stories like these tend to reside in the forefront of our minds.

This story may have to do with your family of origin, a current or past relationship, your chosen career, your body or health issues, your children or lack thereof, etc. Once you have identified your story, write down the main themes of it in your journal.

Now it's time to take action on the Warrior Goddess path. In the space following your story, consciously rewrite the story by taking a perspective that views your past experience as something that ultimately served your highest good. If you are stuck here, one way to start is by listing some good things that have come out of the events you describe above. (In my own example, my family's constant moving was an opportunity for me to experience many different cultures and perspectives.)

Here are a couple other examples.

One of my students discovered that her husband was having an affair. As she stayed present with her shock and upset, she opened to what other story might be possible besides the betrayal and worst-case scenario stories her mind was starting to run. She woke up in the morning with a new storyline that made her actually feel excited: "Now my husband and I get to work on our marriage!" She realized that they had been neglecting their relationship, and with this new information she was motivated to put the energy necessary into her relationship to make it thrive. Her old story was "I did something wrong, this is the worst thing that could have ever happened, how could he have betrayed me?" Her new story was "This affair is the needed catalyst for us to talk about what was not working and what needed to be attended to in order to have a solid relationship."

I just spoke with Judith, a friend of mine who is going through a scary health challenge, and her conscious story writing honoring her fears inspired me. She is an elder in a Native American tradition. One of her favorite practices is the vision quest, a sacred journey into nature with no (or very little) food or water with the intent to seek a vision, or deep spiritual insight, for yourself and to bring back to your community. She realized that when she focused on her health challenge from the old story of victim—"Why me, what did I do wrong, what is going to happen to me?"—she felt helpless and overwhelmed. But when she retold the story and held her experience as a vision quest, she felt powerful, that she was going into the wild to find healing for herself and wisdom for her tribe. She knows that she will continue to feel scared sometimes, but now she is holding her experience in a much larger, and more empowering, story.

Now rewrite your own!

Freeing ourselves from the stories that cause inner suffering is key to being grounded in our Warrior Goddess power.

One thing I hope you noticed in this exercise is that transformation starts with how we use our words—how we speak our story to others and ourselves.

When don Miguel says, "Be impeccable with your word," in *The Four Agreements*, he is sharing an ancient Toltec principle: Be impeccable with your energy, which translates to "Be mindful of what you are doing with your energy through your words *and* actions."

Now let's go deeper and bravely explore where old ancestral and familial roots may be caught up in stories that don't serve who you are today.

Taking Responsibility for Your Family Story

Most of us have some deep-rooted story about our family of origin that needs examination and releasing. For many of us, this story has to do with our parents, but it could also include grandparents, aunts, uncles, or even siblings. For those of you who were adopted or raised by a foster family, work with your adoptive parents or the people who were your primary caregivers and had the most impact on you growing up.

As a child, you soaked up the behaviors and actions of your parents or the people who raised you. Your parents or caregivers did not need to teach you your beliefs and how to react in the world. As a little kid you were like a sponge, soaking in the information around you, which includes not just behaviors, but also the energy of those around you. The energetic patterning, or the sum of experiences that are stored in the body, mind, and emotions of your parents, grandparents, and their grandparents, is passed on to you. So you receive all of their gifts and all of their baggage. Baggage includes any experiences from the past that your family is still unconsciously carrying around, like a heavy suitcase packed with fear, trauma, and unconscious agreements. We want to honor and nurture the many gifts of our lineage and from a compassionate witness space start cleaning up the baggage.

Now you might be saying, "But that is my parents' baggage! Why do I have to clean it? That's not fair. I'm not responsible!" Or you might feel, "My parents (uncle/sister/stepdad/mom who gave you up for adoption) are to blame for ruining my life or making me the neurotic mess that I am."

The truth is that if you discover that you are carrying forward the energetic patterns of old agreements or habits from your parents, alive or dead, that means they now belong to you, and you are responsible for them. *Responsibility* is a wonderful word. Responsibility does not mean you are to blame or you should be punished, but that you have the opportunity to change something if you want to. You don't have to wait for your parents to change or fix anything or be different. You are empowered to take action and free yourself, letting your parents be exactly who they are.

You can also let go of any blame you are holding toward your family. They did the best they could. They were acting from what they learned.

Remember, no matter what abuse you may have experienced, it was not your fault. You are not responsible for other people's actions. You are responsible for whatever agreements and beliefs you carry from your childhood experiences. Once you let go of making others wrong or trying to figure out why something happened, you can start writing a new story and start a new chapter in your life. With love, shift your attention from blame and feeling victimized to giving yourself all the tools and support possible to heal and ground yourself in the present. Even if you had a fabulous, supportive childhood, stay open to what unconscious patterns you might have picked up.

To begin the process of release, begin noticing with curiosity what energy and actions may have traveled down your family lines to you. The best place to start is from a place of gratitude. Separate out your judgment and emotions around your biological or adoptive family to simply honor what positive modeling you did get. Take a few moments to write down five things you appreciate about your parents (or the beings who raised you). Write a list for each parent or major caregiver of at least five things you appreciate. Here is what I brainstormed for my parents:

Mom: her courage, her willingness to travel, her ability to put up with my father when he is grumpy, her love of horses, and her love of humans and the many ways she has volunteered and made a difference in people's lives.

Dad: his incredible will, his vision, his competitive joy in playing racket sports, his financial support so we could travel all over the place, and the many times he came and watched me compete in track.

Now write down five things you took on that you would like to release. What beliefs did your mom or dad or the people that raised you hold that you still act from unconsciously? What did you take on from your parents that you can release?

Be willing to look at yourself and your behaviors and see where you picked them up. Some may be blatant, while others may be more subtle:

Mom: I carried on these patterns: her armoring, her shyness, her belief that she had to take care of others and not herself, her nitpicking at others, and her sense of guilt.

Dad: I carried on these patterns: his stubbornness, his going silent when he was upset with someone, his need to be right, his desire to distract, and his desire to control situations.

The key to releasing old family patterns is to recognize they are simply passed down unconsciously, and now you are becoming conscious of them. Bless them. Then feel into what you need to do in your life to create a sense of stability and rootedness that is not based in your family patterns.

If you have emotions arise while you are releasing these family patterns, let them move! The work is not to suppress your emotions so you can be neutral, but to clear them out so they are released. You do not need to go hunting for emotions; let them arise as they will, and express them in safe ways that will release them, not create more drama. This process may take a long time; do not expect to be done with your parental clearing in one session. But get the ball rolling and see what arises. Just your awareness of your family patterns will begin the clearing process. Then you can begin to claim what you love, and to sink your roots deeper into the things that bring you joy.

The next level of exploration is to bring healing to your family's past. In genealogy we describe our ancestral lines as a family tree. You are the fruit of this tree, and you can become sweeter or more bitter depending on your relation to your roots. I've found that repressing or ignoring the pain and suffering in our biological roots doesn't heal this ancestral tree of life, but actually allows the bitterness of past hate, fear, and anxiety to live on in your being, buried under layers of armoring and expressing itself in unexpected and unpleasant ways. When we begin to witness our own ancestral roots with the water of compassion and understanding, we cleanse the hurtful or toxic patterns that are unconsciously passed down through the generations.

When we look back at the history and possible experiences of our ancestors we build our understanding of the whole tree. By bringing the clear light of our witness to the past with the intent for releasing we create the freedom to choose to say a full-bodied no to what we no longer want to carry forward and an inviting yes to what gifts we do want to bring into the future.

What are some of the traumas of your lineage that you might be carrying? What did your grandparents or great-grandparents experience that you might still carry forward in your energy body? You don't have to carry any trauma or abuse or struggle forward; acknowledge it to bring it into the light of the present. We release past ancestral trauma by naming the challenges and calling on the strengths. Your people survived to create you. You are proof that your ancestors were resourceful, creative, and determined. You are proof of love passed down heart to heart, through generations. Even if your being was conceived in an act of violence, or there was force and abuse in your ancestral lines, eons of instinctual, deep mama and papa love surrounds and negates any actions from fear. Linda Hogan summed up the relationship we can cultivate with our ancestors in this way: "Walking, I am listening to a deeper way. Suddenly all my ancestors are behind me. Be still, they say. Watch and listen. You are the result of the love of thousands."

Tap into this chain of love by tapping directly into the wisdom and gifts of your ancestors. One fabulous place to get help with generational clearing is from our ancestors themselves.

Bring the Gifts Forward by Honoring Your Ancestors

In many different cultures around the world, ancestors are revered, remembered, and referenced. The Samoans bury their parents in their front yard so they can say hi to them every day. Mexicans have a joyous, colorful celebration each year, the Day of the Dead, and visit the cemetery to picnic with their dearly departed, bringing them food and alcohol. On their New Year, many Chinese clean the graves of departed relatives, and many pray daily to tiny altars in their homes dedicated to their ancestors. Some African tribes are horrified at the thought of making a community decision without first calling in the ancestors to get their support and advice.

While it is fairly common to honor or even talk to immediate family members who have passed on, the idea of connecting with dead ancestors, especially dead people we didn't know or didn't like when they were alive, is not high on the priority list of things to do today for many modern women. From a Warrior Goddess point of view, we welcome all resources, whether in spirit form or breathing. This sometimes takes a little brain rewiring. We have to let go of believing that the only insight or guidance relevant to us comes from the living, and also have a willingness to forgive and choose to look for the good in those who have passed. Most of us are open to the idea that those we knew when they were alive are watching over us, but let's not forget the generations that came before them.

I never knew my maternal grandmother; she died long before I was born. I thought it was crazy talk when the idea was first presented to me that I could still be in a relationship with her. She was long dead—how could I get to know her? But just by opening that doorway of possibility, I found that I did have a relationship with my deceased grandma. When I listened I could feel her presence, and sometimes she spoke to me, encouraging me on my spiritual path or inviting me to listen more deeply to my heart. Mostly I feel the essence of who she was, and how similar we are. I am her blood; her DNA gives me life.

By simply being willing to create connection with a known or unknown ancestor, you will find yourself part of a ribbon of women and men who want you to go beyond where they could go.

Lesson Four Resources

Gifts
- You are an energetic being, and just like electricity, your energy runs best when you are grounded to the earth.
- You create a false sense of safety when you connect your well-being to roles, people, or things.

- Freedom comes when you release old ancestral patterns and beliefs, and reclaim your trust in your authentic expression.

- When you bless and honor your ancestors, you carry forward their wisdom and gifts.

Explorations

One beautiful way to honor your ancestors is to create an ancestral altar. This is a place to honor your ancestors and send them your gratitude for your life. Things you can bring to your altar include pictures, candles, family heirlooms or objects, family crests or cloths, flowers, or things you love from nature. You can also make an altar specifically for one family member who loved and supported you. Sit at this altar for a few minutes today, and listen to what guidance or wisdom comes through.

Energize Your Sexuality and Creativity

So I say, if you are burning, burn. If you can stand it, the shame will burn away and leave you shining, radiant, and righteously shameless.

—Elizabeth Cunningham

When I first started on a Warrior Goddess path of healing, I was initially very resistant to even looking at my beliefs on sexuality. In my mind, I was on a spiritual path, and I did not have time to waste on such trivial things as healing decades of gunk around my sexuality. "I'm just fine, thank you very much!" was my motto when it came to sex.

But when I unwound the knots and mended the leaks of my own internal sexual flow, I did myself the kind favor of returning my own energy to myself. I'll share more about my journey later in this chapter. First, let's get an overview of the terrain we will be walking together.

A tremendous amount of confusion, fear, distortion, and wounding resides around the topic of sex in our culture. Many women have been wounded in some fashion by sexuality—simply being surrounded by so many advertisements showing us what it means to be sexy and so many old-school taboos on women being sexual is detrimental to us claiming our own body and sexual nature.

There are many ways that we squash our sacred sexual juiciness. We are taught so many stories about sexuality: It is dangerous. It will get us into trouble. It is shameful. It is not spiritual. We will get hurt. We will be rejected. We will be seen as promiscuous. It is too much. It is not enough. I'm too old for that.

Sometimes when we start on a spiritual path, we consciously or unconsciously bypass looking at our sexual nature, believing it will hinder our growth. On the Warrior Goddess path, the opposite is true; becoming the woman you are meant to be requires a reevaluation of your ideas and beliefs about sex.

Many people are confused about what sexuality is. If you listen to other people's stories about sexual energy (and the stories in your own head), you will hear two interesting core fibs.

One is that sexuality is dirty and sinful. To encapsulate this little white lie: Your sexuality must be controlled or you will become like an animal, humping everything that moves and destroying civilizations in the wake of your carnal lust until you burn in hell forever. (You may laugh, but it is somewhat horrifying how much of this we each carry within us.)

The second fib is that the only way to get anything in life is through wearing your sex on your sleeve. To encapsulate this second little white lie: In order to be popular, noticed, appreciated, find a mate, and obtain material possessions, you must exude copious amounts of sexual come-hither vibes and wear scant clothing that shows off your wares. (For more information, open a magazine, look at a billboard, or turn on your TV.)

I invite you to toss all your stories about sex, and everyone else's stories about sex, into the nearest trash can.

Now, let's start from the beginning with the information I wish we had all learned in a loving way sometime before the third grade. First, sexual energy is a potent force of nature that flows through the birds and the bees and the flowers and the trees, and through you. It is a pure-as-snow, core energy that dances through all two-leggeds, four-leggeds, creepy crawlies, swimmers, and every plant from seed to blossom to fruit. It's not wrong, dirty, immoral, or amoral. It is the central driving force of creation on the planet. Good sex takes us out of our mind and into the beautiful pleasures of the body, it liberates constrictions and blockages, and it softens our habitual armoring. Great sex blasts us out of our personality and into our soul and our connection to all of life.

Sometimes it is hot and insistent like fire; sometimes it flows like the ocean on a windless day. Your breath enhances its playful power, while fear and stress shut it down. Your sexuality is one of the Divine's best gifts for you and the lucky people in your life with whom you choose to share it.

Sexual energy forms the deep roots of your creativity and passion. It is the flowering branches of the sensual enjoyment of your body and senses.

Your sexuality is sacred, and it is highly individual. All types of sexual expression are beautiful when there is conscious consent. Learn about your own sexual flow and energy first, and then play with others as you feel guided.

Never do something you don't want to do. Stay with your experience and pacing, not another's desire or need. Sex is not a prize to give out or a weapon to withhold.

Being a Warrior Goddess does not mean being pious or nonsexual. Being a Warrior Goddess is about having full access to all of your energy, including your sexuality. The High Priestess in the tarot is called "virgin" not because she is not sexual, but because her sexuality is for her; she is sovereign. This means that when she is sexual with others she does not cord or allow herself to be corded. She does not use her sexuality to manipulate or hook other people. She is never sexual out of obligation or caretaking. Her sexuality is sacred, and she loves her own fire! Her path is about igniting her passion for her own sake, honoring her sexual nature, and healing/clearing fear or any beliefs that dampen her access to her life-force.

This does not mean you must be in a traditional partnership. You may be married. And you may choose to be celibate, or be in a time of not being in a relationship. You may have lovers or friends you can explore with. When you're learning how to tap into your sexual energy, it makes no difference whether you have a long-time sexual partner, no lovers, or dozens of lovers. Your goal is to reclaim your sexual life-force in the way that is right for you.

Two areas to attend to around your sexuality are your body image and fear of power. If you are ashamed or uncomfortable with your physical form, this can have an impact on your connection to your sexual flow.

One of my favorite ways to transform our relationship with our body and sexuality comes from Marion Woodman, one of the most widely read authors on feminine psychology. She invites us to dance naked in front of a mirror every day until we have released hatred or embarrassment, and come to see the sacredness of our body. When we stop looking at magazines and commercials and comparing ourselves to who we think we should be, we can show up with the body we have and be in gratitude for our body's capacity to receive pleasure, regardless of our weight or age. This movement toward loving the body we have helps us to listen to what our body needs to be the healthiest it can be, rather than wishing it were different.

Sexuality is also often connected to a fear of our power. Often as little girls we are trained to tone down our vibrancy and sass, and we sometimes learn to fear our own energy and wildness. Your sexuality is powerful, because it is life energy flowing through you. As you reclaim your sexuality for yourself, you will become more confident. You'll get clear about what you want and what you don't want in the bedroom and every other room in your life. You'll find your voice, respect yourself, and lose your fear of being too much or not enough. It might be scary at times, but as a Warrior Goddess your power comes as you claim your sexuality for you. When you access its flow, it will bring incredible movement into all areas of your life.

Here's how to take the next steps in owning your sexuality, sensuality, and creative fire.

Run Sexual Experiments

Whether you are single or partnered, sexual experimentation is a powerful pathway to divine connection and healing. You can run experiments to get clear about what you like, to explore something new, or to move energy in new ways. Experiments range from taking yourself out to a sensual meal, to asking your spouse to play out a fantasy, to asking your lover to spend thirty minutes going down on you. Feel into what you would like to explore in your sexuality, and then design an experiment. Creativity is a big factor here—don't hold back!

Experiments keep you growing and will show you the places that need to be healed, and the places where you can create a lot more flow. By setting aside sacred time for sex dates, you create space in your life to go deeper and open beyond where you have been in the past.

If you do not currently have a sexual partner, and even if you do, I highly recommend that you make sex dates with yourself to experiment with self-pleasuring. Really slow down and let yourself receive and open. Name out loud what you want, so you get some good practice!

Before you start any sexual experiment, get clear first on what your intent is. Why do you want to run more sexual energy? What are you ready to clear out of your being? How do you want to connect with your womb? Always remember that sexual energy is life energy. Growing your sexual capacity and pleasure will bring more creativity, vibrancy, and joy into every aspect of your life.

Honor where you are at, and use experiments to push your edge, without pushing yourself over the edge! You will know when you've gone too far when you leave your body or shut down. Back up and figure out what you can do, rather than focusing on the discomfort of having gone too far. You may want to search for a sex partner to run experiments with. You do not have to be in a committed relationship to explore your sexuality; it is often not too difficult to find a playmate. See the Warrior Goddess Resources section for more information on dating, finding sex partners, and the all-important safe sex talk.

What brings out and activates your sexual nature? Clothes? Music? Nature? For instance, one of my students realized that she felt most sensual when she was dressed to work in the garden. Another shared how much she loves wearing lingerie under her work suit. Let go of old ideas, and feel into what brings you a sense of sacred sensuality and pleasure.

Now, notice if you were triggered in any place reading this chapter. What is your mind saying to you? Explore your reactions and with curiosity notice what your beliefs are around sexuality. Anything that needs to be cleaned up, go to it!

Let me share this part of my journey back to wholeness with you. My hope is that you will see the immense value in being courageous and taking the time to fully heal and reclaim your beautiful, innate sexual flow—for *you*, and not anyone else.

Early in my life, I severely limited the river of my sexuality. I created an internal logjam of beliefs and fears: "If I own my sexual energy, people will see me as a slut," or "It is not spiritual to be sexual."

I had many partners and a few lovers along the way, but each new relationship unfolded in a predictable way. The sacred river of my sexuality would overflow the banks for a few months, but soon it would dry up, and I would return to my structured pattern with my sexual energy. I'd start out with a lot of sexual enthusiasm and excitement, and then I'd find myself closing down, not wanting to be sexual because when I did I'd start weeping uncontrollably or find myself swamped by unnameable fear. Since I didn't understand what was happening, I shut down my sexual energy and dammed up the flow.

I envied women who were in their power and owned their sexuality, but I couldn't imagine I would ever be one of them. When I stopped to admit it to myself, at a very deep level, I felt broken inside.

I don't feel broken anymore. Here is how I made the change.

It started with a surprising ultimatum I made with myself. (The healing technically started much, much earlier, but the ultimatum kicked things into high gear.)

It was the beginning of a new millennium, I was in the process of separating from a three-year intimate relationship, and I could feel in my bones that the time was ripe for something new.

Little did I know that the upcoming change would involve me facing some of my biggest fears.

It started the day I sat down and had a Warrior Goddess heart-to-heart with Spirit—the divine, creative, invisible force that many call God and that I believe is neutral of gender but takes many forms and has many manifestations.

"OK, I'm ready to make some big changes," I said out loud to an empty room, knowing that I was being heard loud and clear by the Divine. "I don't want to keep repeating my old relationship patterns. I would rather be alone than be with someone who does not 100 percent support me to be my best self. I am ready to stop blaming others and to stop blaming myself. I want to change. Tell me what to do next."

I swear, I could hear Spirit gleefully jumping up and down and giggling with delight. And then I was suddenly filled with this knowing:

It was time for me to focus on healing my relationship with my sexuality.

Over the next couple of days, I stubbornly argued with All-That-Is, even though I already knew the truth. Finally, I surrendered and said to God/Goddess, "OK! Yes! I will focus on healing my relationship with my sexuality. Please help me. I'm scared, and I don't know how to do this." The support and guidance I needed appeared, just as I know it will for you when you are ready to heal and reclaim your sexual flow.

Here are some of the steps I took along the way. I read a lot of juicy women's erotica to see what opened me. I watched good, women-created pornography to see what opened me. I unabashedly talked to a lot of women about their sexuality and experiences. I learned to masturbate slowly and see what my body liked. I put my healing before anything else. I found lovers who supported my healing, who didn't need me to be any certain way, and who challenged me to see that I was, indeed, not broken. I found allies, people who shared their healing journey with me. By having other people I could talk to about challenging or even taboo subjects, I learned how similar we all are. Often, the shameful or confusing experiences I thought I was alone in having were actually shared by others. I learned from other women's healing journeys that it was possible to heal and come to love my sexuality.

From my heart to yours: No matter how much debris or how many dams you have created to stay safe, you can reclaim your sacred sexual tides. Flow is your nature. No one can take your sexual essence away, and it can never be broken. The waters of your sexuality can be seemingly polluted momentarily, but the water can always be brought back to its pure state. Always. No exceptions.

Healing and reclaiming your sexuality involves using lots of internal soap and water to gently wash your sexual energy of past trauma, misconceptions, repression, and fear. Keep cleaning with love until the original, innocent, precious nature of your sexual life-force emerges like a laughing baby from the bath. What you will find with the eyes of innocence is that your sexuality is pure life-force, and a magical connection to child-like, playful creativity.

Conscious Creation

Your sexual energy is also your creative energy. You can use sex to reproduce, a most creative act. And you can also take the fiery energy of your sexuality and channel it into catalyzing and birthing anything, from books to careers, health to spiritual practice. At its core your sexual energy is your creative flow, and when you choose to channel it, everything becomes your art.

There is a big difference between unconsciously spreading sexual energy around and consciously accessing the vital life-force we are all blessed with at birth. One is an unclean expression of need, a way to feel loved through our sexuality. The other is a powerful claiming of our birthright to pleasure: the pleasure of sex and the pleasure of creation, in all forms.

When you own your sexuality as your inner fire, you release it from being focused on your genitals and on the physical act of sex, and free it to bring passion into all areas of your life. Instead of "I'm feeling sexual; I need to act on or get rid of this energy," you shift to "I'm feeling sexual; where can I channel this energy?" And whether you are gardening, singing, painting, dancing, or knitting, you can bring more vitality and heat to your activities when you let your sexual, life-force energy flow through your hands and heart.

Warrior Goddesses are creative beings; I believe we have a need to express ourselves in our own unique way. This can be through cooking, our choice of clothing, painting, the artistry in how we raise our children, photography, or our blog. It is about finding what we are passionate about, what lights our inner fire and makes us feel sparkly inside. Creativity is an elixir of life. It keeps us from being dried up and brittle by keeping the essence of our life-force juiciness channeling into new ideas, projects, and visions.

Don't be afraid of your passions. Allow them to fill you up and inspire you. I'm talking about your deepest desire for connection, the space where you open to the Divine in a way that nourishes your soul and makes you feel most alive. If you don't have a creative outlet yet, keep seeking one that lights you up from the inside out. Don't wait. Step toward what makes you feel the most yummy, from dancing to waterskiing to gardening.

Lesson Five Resources

Gifts

- Your sexuality is life-force energy, connected to your creativity, vitality, and joy.

- Whether you are celibate, partnered, or have many lovers, reclaiming and healing your relationship to your sexuality is one of the biggest gifts you can give yourself.

- Be willing to discover *your* sexual integrity. What lights you up?

- Running sexual experiments with yourself or others is one of the paths to owning your sexuality.

- Your creativity is your access to a fulfilling, nourishing life. Find what you are passionate about and take actions that juice you.

Explorations

Bitty Baby Steps

One really good experiment to run for Warrior Goddess Training is around asking for and receiving what you want. Many women keep themselves feeling safe and under control by giving sexually, but not allowing themselves to surrender to really receiving. Make a date where you surrender to receiving (with a partner or with yourself!). Notice if this is easy or difficult for you. Can you allow yourself to receive pleasure without giving anything back? Can you let yourself surrender control and be pushed a bit past your armoring in order to merge more fully with the Divine? Are you able to ask for what you want in the moment?

Healing from Sexual Abuse

Many women are sexually abused as children or adults, and so choose to clamp down on their sexual energy. Sometimes being sexual brings up old trauma or memories, or causes women to disassociate. To heal from old wounding, it is important to consciously clear the perpetrator out of your womb. Use your breath to bring love and acceptance into the places that have been hurt, and release any energy that doesn't belong to you. Pay attention to any ways that you are abusive to yourself, such as being too rough or having sex when you don't want to. Change your behaviors to match your intent: to bring loving touch and healing to yourself, not more trauma.

You can heal. It simply takes patience, a desire to no longer be a victim. Give yourself positive, fun sexual experiences. If emotion arises when you are being sexual, simply allow yourself to move through the feelings. You don't need to know where the emotions came from; just let them flow. If memories arise or you start leaving your body, stop and ask for what you need—to be held, for the lights to be turned on, etc. It is very helpful to work with a loving partner and connect with them eye-to-eye and heart-to-heart often.

Exercise: Cultivating Creativity

I often do this process as a paired exercise in workshops. It works great when done alone, but it is even more expansive with a creative friend.

Pick an issue you are working on and play with new solutions. Start by breathing into your low belly and calling in some life-force creative energy. Then brainstorm at least five creative solutions to your problem with no limit on how realistic they have to be. Don't think; write them down without editing or backtracking. For this exercise, the more outrageous your ideas, the more your brain will open to come up with creative solutions that will support you.

Here are a couple creative brainstorming examples. You'll see that some creative brainstorms are simple, while some are more on the crazy side. Write them all down, then review for possible actions.

Problem: My relationship just ended, and I want do things in a new way.

Creative brainstorming:

- Have a divorce celebration at a fun venue with some close friends to support me.

- Spend a week in retreat, nourishing myself with good food and plenty of long hikes.

- Take my new alone time to do something I have always dreamed of trying, such as scuba diving or pottery.

- Get on the Internet, create a personal ad, and then go on dates with fifteen people in four weeks with the agreement that I will not get into a relationship but simply explore what I like or how I am around others.

- Shave my head and dedicate myself to meditation for a year.

- Volunteer to help a child in need.

- Find a good therapist or spiritual guide.

Problem: I am having a hard time getting my teenage son out of bed in the mornings, and it is creating a lot of stress in the household.

Creative brainstorming:

- Get his little sister to wake him up every morning with ice.
- Buy him an alarm clock and tell him he is on his own to get himself up.
- Have him go to bed fully dressed with everything ready.
- Hire a marching band to play outside of his window every morning until he gets out of bed.
- Tell him he doesn't have to go to school anymore. He can take the GED whenever he wants to.
- Tell him he has to sleep at school.
- Ask him what would help him get out of bed.

As you brainstorm both inside the lines and outside of the lines, new possibilities will open up. Keep breathing into your belly, connecting to your creative life-force and stretching your brain toward the outrageous. Then when you review your list you will probably see a new solution.

Notice what you typically do, and seek what would be different from your usual pattern. Be creative! The best actions to help you return to integrity come from the wellspring of creativity that you possess. Be playful as you dream up ways to experiment and take action.

Claim Your Strength and Ignite Your Will

*There are only two types of women—
goddesses and doormats.*

—Pablo Picasso

I used to be more of a doormat than a goddess. It started with my first proper boyfriend, when I was sixteen years old. We had just moved to Singapore and I was in my invisible first year there, coming in as a shy junior. I was shocked that he noticed me at all. That he not only noticed me, but liked me, was overwhelmingly intoxicating. I felt like a princess, finally seen through my braces and glasses and gawky awkwardness.

I wanted him to like me so thoroughly that his will became my will. Whatever he wanted, I did without question. I was the ultimate pleaser, always putting his well-being before my own. I wanted to be liked, so I tried to be who I thought he would like best. In doing so, I used my power to become what I thought I should be, instead of using my energy to find out who I was and what I liked.

Of course, even after this first relationship ended, my pattern of pleasing continued to weave through all aspects of my life, from work to relationships, friendships to personal decisions. It is oh-so-easy for us as women to give our choice and our power away to others without realizing the damage we do to ourselves. But once we see this old pattern, we can start to gather back the scattered seeds of our power and learn to nourish ourselves back into our own steadiness.

As we talked about in the first Warrior Goddess lesson, Commit to You, true power does not come from outside people, places, or things, but from within. To reclaim your strength you must be honest about where you have linked your power outside of yourself, and where you are seeking safety in old strategies rather than conscious action.

Igniting your will occurs when you are clear on what you really want for yourself, and when you take action based on this knowledge. If you are consumed with what others think, you are repressing your fears, and you will not have the will needed to stand in your power.

So the first step to claiming your strength and igniting your will is to get clear about what you want. Not what your victim wants, or what your judge wants, or what you would like, but what your highest vision and purpose is for yourself. What I have found is that when you get clear about your heart's desire, the Universe steps up in magnificent ways to support you!

Let's find out what you really want in the major areas of your life. On a separate sheet of paper, write down the answers to the following questions. Don't spend too long thinking about your answers, or you risk succumbing to the judge or victim. It doesn't matter if a voice in your head yells, "That isn't realistic" as you write down your answers; the point here is to let your true desires spill out.

- What do you want your most intimate relationships to look like? (This can include others and/or yourself.)

  ○ My response: *I want my intimate relationships to be based in honesty, respect, and compassion, and I want to be supportive and loving toward myself, even when I make a mistake.*

- What do you want your career to look like? (Remember, staying at home with the kids is a big-time job!)

  ○ My response: *I want to write a book a year, have a balanced home and travel life, and share the teachings with many people to help foster transformation and open space for more love and creativity in the world.*

- What do you want the relationships with your family and friends to look like? (Imagine a place of trust and nonjudgment, remembering that we cannot receive what we are unable to give.)

  ○ My response: *I want to have the time to play and celebrate with my friends and family.*

- What do you want your free time to look like? (Do you want to dance more? Spend more time learning? Travel?)

  ○ My response: *I want to spend more time singing and in nature. I want to stay steady with my spiritual practices and exercise in a way that makes my body feel strong and healthy.*

Don't edit as you write—just see what comes through. Being clear about what you want is a major start to getting it.

Note: Sometimes life presents us with situations that prevent us from pursuing what we really want in the present moment. For instance, I have a friend who would really like to be living in

Europe right now, but her mother is elderly and in poor health. She has chosen to stay in the United States with her mother for the time being to help her through life's final transition. So while a part of my friend would like to be living someplace else, she consciously chooses to stay here for now, recognizing that she wants to take care of her mother more than she wants to be in Italy. She is conscious not to tell herself any victim stories around her choice. She also knows that at some point it is likely she will be able to pursue her dream of living abroad.

Getting Back to Authentic Action

As we learn what we really want, many of us realize that we have actually misused our will up until this point in our lives.

Most likely you have learned to use your will for one main purpose: to stay safe. There are many ways we create a (false) sense of safety:

- by trying to change and manipulate our environment (*controlling*)
- by bouncing from thing to thing (*distracting*)
- by hiding and pretending to be small (*isolating*)
- by making sure others like us (*pleasing*)

I call these four ways of being our core strategies. I first wrote about these strategies in one of my first books, *Spiritual Integrity*, with my coauthor Raven Smith. Here is a synopsis of how our strategies sap our strength, and how to take back our power from them.

Our Core Strategies for Coping

As women, most of us have a bit of all four strategies working within us. We also have a whole lot of one of them within us. Your core strategy is your go-to response, which gives you a sense of power when you feel scared or confused.

The purpose of your core strategy is to keep the world manageable and to create a sense of safety and stability.

Controllers

Controllers feel safe when they are in control of the world around them or their own internal world. Controllers can be great leaders and visionaries, but often their gift is used to squash uncomfortable situations, to force people to do what they want them to do, and to limit expression. Controllers manage their own and others' emotions through subtle or blatant domination or manipulation. They believe their way is the right way.

Distractors

Distractors keep themselves safe by staying busy and checked out. Instead of feeling their feelings or facing discomfort, distractors spend hours playing video games, doing projects/hobbies, talking to friends, seeking out anything that can be a distraction! Distractors have a great gift of multitasking and are often mentally nimble, but their energy is easily scattered, and they have a very difficult time focusing and creating what they want in the world.

Isolators

Isolators habitually hide when they are scared or are in an uncomfortable situation. This hiding may be a physical or emotional retreat. When triggered (or before there can be any trigger), isolators head for the safety of the hills. Isolators often have a very strong connection to Spirit and an excellent sense of self, but they are split between a yearning to be deeply seen and understood and a desire to be invisible. They habitually constrict their energy and their choices.

Pleasers

Pleasers believe they will only be accepted and safe when they are helping others. Pleasers constantly scan other people's reactions, wanting to make sure that everyone is happy. Their gifts are sensitivity and an aptitude for sacred service, but when they are in their strategy to keep safe, they become hypervigilant and outer-focused. The result is they often feel victimized and resentful. Pleasers often feel lost when they are not caretaking or acting to satisfy the perceived needs of others.

How do you react to stressful situations? Do you take control, suddenly find something else is more important, isolate yourself, or caretake and please others? Look for your core strategy, the one you default to when you are surprised or overwhelmed.

If you are like most people, there is a part of you that doesn't want to change, that is invested in the strategy you have created, and that believes fully that your strategy will keep you "safe." Your core strategy is so woven into the fabric of your being that it will take focused action to untangle what is your true authentic power and what is a strategy.

Here's an exploration. Spend the next few days witnessing your strategy. How does it play out in your life? How does it affect you? Play with being inspired by the brilliance of your strategy, not overwhelmed by its strength. Notice how it served you in the past, knowing as you gain awareness of the ins and outs of your strategy that you are gaining power over it.

Ask yourself: Am I willing to learn to live beyond my strategy? Am I willing to take the risk to do what needs to be done so I can live from my integrity in every aspect of my life? What do I need to do to cultivate more willingness?

Often when you begin to unravel your strategy, the response is: But how else could I act? What should I do? Your perception can become so narrowed by your core strategy that you often see no other options of how to be; you have mistaken this core strategy for who you are. And as you start to challenge the strategy, you can feel insecure and out of control. This is where willingness comes in. Instead of becoming overwhelmed and confused, you can learn to consciously cultivate your desire to live as a Warrior Goddess, beyond strategies. Your willingness will be the fuel as you untangle your strategies and learn new channels of behavior.

By cultivating conscious willingness, you will stay steady through the uncomfortable places as you unravel your authentic choice from your strategies. Willingness does not mean that you have it all figured out or that you know what comes next. Willingness is a state of opening to anything that arises and staying present with whatever your mind, emotions, and body are doing.

True willingness has to begin somewhere, and that somewhere is the truth. Not where you *wish* you were or think you *should* be, but where you really are in this moment. You need to be truly willing to tell yourself the truth about what you want to transform in your life.

As a Warrior Goddess, your strength is in embracing the challenges of life, loving all of you including your weaknesses, and saying yes to discomfort. This does not mean seeking out drama or difficult situations, but using everything in your life to foster more resilience, courage, and core strength.

I recently heard about some new studies on stress that challenge everything we've been told about how stress is bad for us. This new research suggests that stress might actually be good for you, as it helps build strength and focus when it is needed most. Health psychologist Kelly McGonigal believes the harmful effects of stress may be a consequence of our perception that it is bad for our health, but the stress itself is not inherently bad. Nature seems to have the same message for us Warrior Goddesses: You can use your environment and experiences to gain strength and resiliency.

When steel is tempered, heat and pressure are used to strengthen the metal. When a butterfly first begins to emerge from its cocoon, it must struggle in order to strengthen its wings. If someone frees the butterfly from its cocoon prematurely, it will not be able to fly because its crucial tempering stage will not have occurred. In one experiment where an entire ecosystem was created within a protected bubble, the healthy trees fell unexpectedly. Researchers later realized that these trees needed wind in order build their structural strength to stay upright.

If we try to avoid the hard work of breaking down our old confining structures or if we make other people responsible for our own freedom, we will not have what it takes to truly inhabit our essential nature. When we stand in our own center, the challenges we encounter temper us. We can see our inner and external struggles as the cocoon or the wind, the very thing that will strengthen our wings and let our branches reach up to the sky.

I've found that when I am in a tough situation, such as under a deadline or in a hard emotional place, if I can focus on being creative and curious about how I am being tempered or strengthened, I thrive. Artists often say that scarcity, tension, and time constraints can improve their work. Explore shifting your attitude so all your challenging experiences can foster your power and flexibility, and allow you to spread your wings wide. True Warrior Goddess strength embraces the difficult, shadow aspects of ourselves. Strength is not about overpowering that which we do not understand or which scares us; it's about learning to courageously work with the energies of life. This is a beautiful internal move, to not use the power of the shadow against ourselves, but as a source of energy.

Pure acceptance and love is the most direct way to tame our internal demons. Anger, judgment, frustration, and fear only feed the destructive elements. When we truly open our heart and move from peaceful stillness, we can befriend our fierceness. We cease trying to govern ourselves or others and choose to creatively direct our emotions and fear. We learn to set clear boundaries and to clarify our expectations with grace and dignity. Strength reflects a strong, conscious container that embraces all parts of self. We are each intimately linked to our desires and feelings, which are not something to ignore or battle. Working with rather than against our self grants us the energy to clear out old wounds to reveal hidden limitations.

When we accept our Warrior Goddess power we stop using other people's opinions against us and focus on improving our opinion of ourselves. We stop taking anything personally, and move past the victim/perpetrator, right/wrong models to step into the power of gentleness and the fierceness of compassion, which exist beyond blame and self-doubt.

Being a goddess means valuing yourself highly. It is an attitude of self-respect and self-love without compromise. Being a Warrior Goddess means being comfortable with both your power and your vulnerability, knowing they are both strengths.

Experimenting Beyond Strategies

Each of the strategies above has a gift, a core strength that when used consciously helps us to align with our authentic power. But to move past using our strategies unconsciously takes discipline. Discipline is not a punishment, but an ally to help us focus and direct our will and attention exactly where we want it to go. I love this quote from empowered fitness guru Patricia Moreno: "Discipline is freedom. It is you getting yourself to do what you really want to do."

One of the best ways to release unconscious strategies and do what you really want to do, respond how you really would like to respond, and act as you really want to act is to run experiments to free up your energy. We want to live authentically, not automatically. This is a shift away from the will of our strategy and into the will of our strength.

These types of experiments are similar to what the Toltec call "not doings." A not doing is an action that you take for no reason except to break old patterns. Some simple examples of not doings are eating with your nondominant hand, driving to work a different way each day, or digging a deep hole and then filling it up again. The goal of not doings is twofold: to help you learn to put 100 percent of yourself into an action for no reward or reason, and to shake up habitual ways of being.

Since strategies are unconscious habits, not doings are a great way to create more fluidity and choice. What we are experimenting with are new ways of taking action. So start by watching your patterns and habits around your strategy. When do you control, distract, isolate, or please? Witness your behaviors and reactions without judging yourself. It can be frustrating to see how often you are acting from strategy rather than authenticity, but stay lighthearted and curious.

A couple of pointers: If you are in any leadership role at work, and even if you are not, we are mostly trained to control as a way of meeting goals. The overall strategy of the work world is control. This might not be your personal strategy, just something you learned how to do at your nine-to-five. Unweaving control as a strategy at work is important in favor of real leadership. Realize that in your personal life you may be a pleaser or an isolator. Name your personal strategy and work on that separately from any other "roles" you have in your life.

In the United States and much of the rest of the world, the overall strategy for coping is distraction. Just look at the popularity of Facebook—it is a distractor's paradise! Or notice the fast pacing, quick edits, and frequent commercial breaks of television, and the movement toward sound bites instead of in-depth information. So while you may have distractor tendencies due to the environment you are in, your personal strategy may be controlling, or isolating, or pleasing. My belief is that all Warrior Goddesses can benefit from decreasing distraction in their lives.

To run an experiment for change, pick a time frame and specific actions. Be clear and precise on what the experiment is you are running, and try to remain open to the outcome. If you believe you already know the result, it is not an experiment, is it? Experiments make it easier to try new things and can help us to stay steady even when what we are doing is challenging.

Here are a couple of ideas for not doings. You set the time frame, and away you go! These are not forever actions, but a way to use your will to come into more choice.

- For controllers: Do an opinion fast. Don't share your point of view, even when you are asked for it. Go into silence. Make a practice of saying, "I was wrong."

- For distractors: Practice regular five-minute focus sessions where you stop and bring your attention to your breath and body. Do one thing at a time. Wait one minute between tasks.

- For isolators: Go out to a gathering or event even if you don't feel like it. Set your intent to meet one new person a day. Go deeper with someone you know and trust by sharing a vulnerability.

- For pleasers: Say no to any requests you receive that you would usually say yes to. When you are at someone else's house, don't do the dishes or extra work. If someone asks you where you want to have lunch, share your opinion.

Any good experiment around shifting strategies is going to be challenging in some way because it will be unfamiliar. Be gentle with yourself. We take on specific strategies often as young children, and it can be surprisingly unnerving when we start to shift them. Stay the course and let the transformation happen.

Our next Warrior Goddess lesson will guide us to dissolve old armoring and let the brilliance of our most inner power shine forth.

Lesson Six Resources

Gifts

- Power comes from deepening our relationship with our innermost guidance.

- Strength comes from stepping toward and loving our fears and weaknesses.

- Old strategies sap our energy and come from trying to keep ourselves safe.

- Using our will and loving discipline to make new choices frees up our creativity and capacity.

Explorations

Listing Strengths

Make a list of what you consider your weaknesses. Then next to each one name how it is also a strength. Look back over your life and write down what events brought you the most self-awareness and sense of inner power. Write down all the things in your life that you have "survived" that made you stronger.

Open Your Heart

Seeking love keeps you from the awareness that you already have it—that you are it.

—Byron Katie

For years I understood the concepts of loving more and unconditional acceptance. I knew the woman I wanted to be: more loving, more accepting, more compassionate. But in day-to-day living I struggled with keeping my heart open, especially when I felt afraid. In my quest to soften my heart I noticed a direct correlation between my heart and my judge: When my own critical voice was loud, my heart closed. Even with this awareness my inner judge continued to torment me, and my heart stayed armored and protected.

Believe it or not, it was a painting of an ancient eagle that catapulted me into a new relationship with my heart. It was 1996, and I was with don Miguel Ruiz and a group at the pyramids of Teotihuacan, Mexico. I was quietly meditating in front of a mural of an eagle when suddenly I had a vision of the eagle leaping out of the wall, grabbing my heart in its beak, and flying to the sun. I had been praying to release my fears around a relationship I was in, and I intuitively knew the message that was being given to me through this vision: Your heart does not belong to you or anyone else; it is of the Universe. Let it shine like the sun. Do not attach your heart to this or that; let your heart be a reflection of the love of the Universe, one that emanates pure light.

I realized in the intense moment of that experience that my authentic heart could not break, or be given away, or belong to one person, or even have preferences. My heart was not a separate organ, but the whole Universe of stars and space pulsing in my chest. I felt and understood how intimately I was connected with everything, and how fiercely I loved all of it! The pleasure, the pain, the suffering, the joy, the lover, the thief, the lady at the checkout stand, my best friend were all sacred, pure love in motion viewed through the eyes of my true heart.

Over time, I realized that in my experience with the eagle at Teotihuacan, a fundamental shift had happened in my being. My center of gravity had moved from my head to my heart. While the judge in my mind could still hook my attention, it was no longer the one who led. Sometime after this experience I made a mistake, and a sweet inner voice said, "Whoops, let's try that again!" I froze in surprise. After years and years of my internal judge pushing me to be better, to try harder, to be perfect, this gentle self-acceptance was unfamiliar.

At first I was suspicious, as if an old enemy had suddenly started bringing me chocolate and sending flowers. Why was I being nice to myself for making a mistake? Was the judge going to return and punish me further down the road? What if my judge was right, and being nice to myself made me soft so I'd make more mistakes, or become complacent?

As I continued to watch the transformation of my inner dialogue from fear (mind) to love (heart), I saw how being motivated by the fearful judge drained my energy and kept me anxious and on edge, while being inspired and guided by my accepting heart helped me feel happier, confident, and more flexible.

Things really started to shift when I started being in a relationship with my mind from my heart. This is an important lesson of a Warrior Goddess heart: Be compassionate and fiercely loving with yourself as you unwind old knots and fears and grow your heart's capacity. We have all had experiences that blast us open to love: the birth of a child, an unexpected spiritual experience, even that perfect color dress. These are all tastes of the heart, dipping into the stream of the heart's power. We want to take these singular experiences and stabilize our heart as our perceptual center. Really living from your heart takes a warrior's tools: patience, perseverance, and humor. So get your compassionate Goddess of Sacred Cleaning and Purification ready to work side by side with your warrior focus to clear any stagnation and false beliefs around your heart.

Purifying Your Heart

Your heart is the strongest muscle in your body, and it will beat 2.5 billion times over your lifetime. Energetically, the heart's ability for giving and receiving is endless. However, for many of us the heart is usually one of our most guarded areas. We have a tendency to armor our hearts if we do not feel secure, if we experience physical, emotional, or sexual trauma, and/or if we do not feel powerful. This is why purifying your vessel, releasing old stories, and claiming your strengths are so important. Not doing these things will leave your heart feeling fragile and vulnerable, and what we perceive as vulnerable we will protect.

We protect our heart in numerous ways: physically by rounding our shoulders and sinking the chest in, emotionally by closing down our access to feelings for fear of pain, and mentally by believing we can be broken or destroyed unless we stay isolated. This type of protection gives us the illusion that we are in control and safe.

The glass barriers we put around our heart cause us to fear being shattered. But the heart is wise and strong beyond measure when we give it space to unfurl. Scientific studies are now proving that the heart has an innate wisdom of its own, not connected to the mind. In their groundbreaking book *The HeartMath Solution*, Doc Childe and Howard Martin draw on over thirty years of scientific research to prove that the heart is not just an organ that pumps blood; it is the true intellectual center of our being. The heart has 40,000 neurons, as many as the brain, and when the heart leads the mind becomes more focused and relaxed. When you consciously activate the intelligence of your heart, your creativity and intuition rise and your stress and anxiety decrease.

So how do you access your heart's wisdom? At its core, your heart is a great teacher and friend. But around this core of truth is a gnarled web of mental lies and fears. When you bring your awareness into the light of your true heart, you can illuminate and release the mental stories that close your heart.

One of the primary heart-armoring beliefs we carry is that people can hurt you. Yes, it is true that your physical body can be hurt. But is your physical body "you"? It is true that your emotional body can be hurt. Is your emotional body "you"? There are many people who are crippled or in emotional pain, but their essence is untouched. If you believe you are only your body or your emotions, you will constantly fear physical or emotional pain. Your armored heart will contract just thinking about the slightest possibility of physical or emotional pain, even if it is not happening! And this is what we spend most of our lives doing, worrying about how we are going to avoid pain and grasping after fleeting pleasures.

When we replay our physical or emotional fears over and over again, we are stuck in our focus on survival. This part of us is vital, but for most modern humans it is way out of balance. Imagine a deer that gets startled by a sound. All of her senses are honed, and she freezes and looks around for danger or flees to safety. If there is not an immediate threat, she is very quickly back to peacefully grazing.

When we link our survival to whether or not we are loveable or dwell on possible physical pain, we stay in fight-or-flight mode. We are constantly on survival high alert for rejection or abandonment or potential pain. Our mental false beliefs run our lives, telling us we are fragile or bad things are going to happen. When we shift to our heart's wisdom we know that we are always held, loved, and supported by the Universe, even if we are struggling in this moment. The mind can then rest into the heart and help us calm our nervous system down or find creative solutions when we feel threatened.

Another big tangle is the notion that there is someone outside who is "the one," the one who will rescue you or love you devotedly or make you whole. We take an unbounded, infinite heart and tell it, "OK, there is only one person you are going to truly love and who can truly love you. So wait until you find this person, and then it will all be OK." This romantic fantasy is hugely prevalent in our culture, especially among women, though it is definitely not limited to females. For some of us, this need to live out a romantic fantasy is so strong that we sometimes enter into relationships that do not serve us. Two of the most common ways we do this are by either settling for a partnership that we know doesn't fulfill us or by staying in relationships that are long dead. Or we may go to the other extreme, blaming this ideology as the cause for us to avoid any type of relationship since we haven't found "the one," and so we feel hopeless and give up (while secretly waiting, waiting, hoping, hoping).

When you live from this romantic fantasy, you put off your own life by waiting for an illusion. Because if you did find "the one" and you have not cleared out your fear and limitations, you will spend the relationship (after the initial bliss wears down a bit) worrying about how you are going to keep it! But the truth of the Warrior Goddess path is that you can only merge with another when you become your own "one" and free your heart from believing it needs outside acceptance, love, or support to be whole.

When you open your understanding to the wider truth that nothing can hurt the real you, and that you need nothing and no one to be complete, you will feel the unbounded, unchangeable, unified spirit that you are. You will choose what type of relationships to be in, not based on fear (I should be in a relationship by now, I better get married so I can have kids, at least it is better than being alone), but rather from a place of unconditional self-love, where you will intuitively know what would best serve you in this time of your life. No part of your heart will need to close down, because you know that your heart can't be broken.

This journey of opening the heart wider than our fears takes time and perseverance, as you have spent years training it to do the opposite. The next time you notice your heart starting to close off or become scared, the medicine to feed yourself is compassion and self-love. Following is an example of what I mean by this.

A friend was driving me to a workshop, and I was having a rough day. When she asked me what was wrong I started to cry and shared all the ways that I was overwhelmed and scared about some changes coming up in my life. Her response was, "OK, Warrior Goddess, you know you always land on your feet. It's time to step up and walk the talk."

In the past my judge would have used my friend's words to say, "Get over your whining and get a grip! What is wrong with you?" Result: closed heart to self, a pushing down of emotions, and attempting to bully myself into making the change.

Or I might have taken her words and said, "No one understands what I am going through. It is all too much and I can't do this!" Result: closed heart to self, and feeling more victimized and overwhelmed.

I chose to take the Warrior Goddess path. I took a deep breath, closed my eyes, and opened my heart to me. From this openhearted place I let myself feel my emotions completely and witnessed what was arising. I felt the overwhelm. I felt my judge's frustration and sense of being out of control. I felt my victim's terror of not doing it right. Then I went inside and soothed the part of me that was scared. "Hi, scared part! There is a lot going on right now, but it is going to be OK. I'm here with you. It's going to be OK." I stopped judging myself and chose to just be present in this moment. This self-compassion created a release in my being, and I could then look for what was working and what were my next steps, all from a loving place. When I opened my eyes again, I told my friend, "OK, I'm ready to go!"

Being a Warrior Goddess does not mean you never have emotional meltdowns, or that you never have a difficult day, or that you avoid heartbreak. Being a Warrior Goddess is about falling in love with all of you: with your judge self, your victim self, and your wise Warrior Goddess self. You are worthy of love, and the heart healing comes when you stop looking outside for love and open to the immense love your heart has for you.

Loving Your Inner Judge and Victim

The most intimate relationship you will ever have is with yourself. But if you don't love every aspect of yourself, then your relationship is out of balance. When the inner judge or inner victim shows up, the path of the Warrior Goddess invites you to love these parts of yourself as well. Compassion is the key to doing so.

Remember, both the judge and the victim are defense mechanisms that were born with the best of intentions—to keep you safe. But the Warrior Goddess path shows us that both the judge and the victim operate from a flawed point of view. They believe that your heart is fragile and can be broken.

The judge whispers to you, "If you did not have me telling you what to do, you would get hurt. You need me to keep others at a distance, to tell you right from wrong."

Right next to your inner judge is your inner victim. It says things like, "It's not fair! This always happens to me!" The victim is the part of you that is crouched in fear, waiting for the next blow to come, or whining and praying someone will come make things better.

When you look deeply at the roles each internal part plays, you'll see the stronger your judge, the stronger your victim. They are two sides of the same coin, that ping-pong back and forth between extremes.

The path of the Warrior Goddess calls us to be aware when the voices of the inner judge or inner victim speak up, acknowledge them for what they are, and then release them with compassion.

Exercise: Noticing the Messages of the Judge and the Victim

Think of the last few months of your life and situations that have arisen. Identify up to three examples where your judge took charge and up to three examples where your victim led the day. For many of us, these areas are repetitive throughout our lives (relationships, career, family, body, etc.). In other words, we consistently self-judge or self-victimize over similar types of situations. By writing them out in your journal, you can better recognize them for what they are the next time they come up, and consciously acknowledge and release them. This means loving these voices as a part of yourself, but choosing to no longer believe the messages they are telling you.

Here's a sample list (Don't think, just write when you do yours!):

Judge: 1. My judge told me I was doing it all wrong for not being more loving when I got frustrated and argued with a friend last week. 2. My judge criticized me when I dropped my favorite glass, telling myself I was clumsy and didn't deserve to have beautiful things. 3. My judge got angry with me when I couldn't make up my mind and compared myself to my brother and how clear he is: Why aren't you as focused and calm as Robert?

Victim: 1. My victim felt overwhelmed and defeated when I didn't get the job, and I felt sorry for myself for all the other places I wasn't picked throughout my life. 2. My victim blamed all my problems on the belief that my sister got more support and love from my parents, which is why I keep picking unhealthy relationships. 3. My victim told me it is OK to eat that second piece of cake because I deserve it for all the difficulties in my life.

When we list out exactly what the judge or victim is saying, we can go into our heart and replay each situation from our heart's intelligence instead of through our mind's stories. How would you rewrite each of the above judge and victim statements? If you want, practice with the judge–victim list above first, and then create your own judge–victim list to rewrite from the heart. With practice, this new heart-centered way of seeing the world will become your reality.

We've learned that the opposite of judgment is discernment. When we discern, we access the clear wisdom of our mind and our heart working together. Contrast this with how quickly your heart closes when the judge appears in any form. This is how you can tell if you are judging rather than discerning: Your heart will clench. An open "I do not like his behavior," or "That was not your best, dear one—let's try again," is very different than "He is a horrible asshole," or "You suck. You blew it again. I knew you would—you can't do anything right."

When the heart speaks through discernment there is compassion, which sometimes can be gentle and sweet, and at other times can be forceful, direct, and cut to the truth instantly. Compassion is not a passive, no-action place, but a powerful, passionate embrace of life stemming from the heart. To unweave the binds around our heart's wisdom and transition from a judging, closed stance to a present, compassionate opening takes practice. By becoming aware of when you are using your judge internally and externally, you will learn to take new action.

Practicing Metta (Loving-Kindness)

There is a beautiful ancient Buddhist meditation called *metta*, or loving-kindness. This is a great Warrior Goddess heart practice that will have a huge impact on your heart. The goal of practicing metta is to help you reverse your programming so you can open your heart rather than close it.

The practice of metta involves four steps. First you start by sending loving-kindness to yourself. Then you send loving-kindness to a family member or dear friend. Next, you send loving-kindness to an acquaintance or someone you are neutral about. The final step is to send loving-kindness to someone you dislike or feel resentful toward.

Sending loving-kindness is kind of like sending someone a blessing, or positive intentions, or a prayer that this person experience only love and bounty in life. As you can imagine, it is much easier to do this for a dear friend or family member than it is someone you dislike.

This begs the question, why would you want to feel loving toward someone you don't agree with? Or toward someone who wronged or betrayed you? Or toward someone doing atrocious acts? Because any energy you send out goes through your own physical, emotional, mental, and spiritual being first. So when you send out judgment, you are feeding yourself judgment. When you send out hatred, you are actually bathing all of your cells in hatred before it goes anywhere. The only outcome of this is more deep-rooted self-hatred and judgment. But when you send out love, you experience that love as well.

For example, after taking the first three steps of metta, I chose a political figure I strongly disliked for step four. I put a picture of this person in my room and practiced metta each time I saw the photo. Because my desire to open my heart was bigger than my desire to hold blame and separation toward another human, I eventually was able to send this person loving-kindness.

Now when I see a photo of this particular person, my heart opens. I still don't agree with him. But I no longer withhold my love to myself by not loving him.

For many women, it's easier to start your metta practice first with someone you love, move to someone you feel neutral about, and then bring loving-kindness to yourself. That's because so often women have deeply buried self-loathing. Practicing loving-kindness with someone who opens your heart first and then with someone you are neutral about lays the groundwork for bringing that same loving-kindness to yourself and gently erasing, layer by layer, any self-rejection or self-hatred.

Exercise: The Heart-Reclaiming Practice of Metta

Start by sending loving-kindness to a dear friend, family member, or pet—anyone that you feel genuine love and gratitude toward. Let the energy build, and feel it moving out and coming back to you. Anchor this feeling in your body.

> **I send loving-kindness to _____. My wish is that he/she experiences only love and happiness in his/her life.**

Next, embody this same sense of loving-kindness toward someone you feel neutral about or toward an acquaintance. Practice cultivating the same amount of loving-kindness that you felt in the first practice.

I send loving-kindness to _____. My wish is that he/she experiences only love and happiness in his/her life.

Next, apply this same wish to yourself. Take your time here, and really envision all the good things you want in your life and watch them come true.

I send loving-kindness to myself. My wish is that I experience only love and happiness in my life.

The next layer is to embody loving-kindness toward someone you dislike. Start with a person you have a mild aversion to.

I send loving-kindness to _____. My wish is that he/she experiences only love and happiness in his/her life.

Only when you are able to consistently send out loving-kindness toward this person should you move on to someone you more actively judge. Eventually you will work yourself to sending loving-kindness toward people you feel you hate or judge fiercely. You may have to work through resistance, fear, and distaste; keep breathing!

The practice of loving-kindness reinforces the idea that it's not our hatred or judgment that brings positive change to the world; it is our presence and capacity to love unconditionally that does so. Choosing to be compassionate toward someone does not mean you agree with his or her actions. It means your authentic heart honors their authentic heart.

Another benefit of metta is that you will begin to unwind the places you feel judged and victimized by others, or where you have judged. As you practice and bring the simple loving presence of your heart forward, separation begins to dissolve and compassionate awareness takes the place of the voices of judgment and victimization.

An important note to all of you with a tendency to people-please: Coming from your heart does not mean you take care of everyone around you. Caretaking is actually a disrespectful habit based out of our unwillingness to be uncomfortable and our arrogance that we know what is best for others. The loving-kindness meditation is a healing Warrior Goddess act of honoring everyone for where they are instead of trying to fix them.

Do this practice over and over again, starting with someone you love, then moving to someone you are neutral about, then to yourself, then to someone you dislike. If you get stuck, go back a step and anchor the feeling of loving-kindness in your heart again. You are rewiring yourself from the inside out, and doing so involves the practice of loving-kindness via this exercise or something like it, not just thinking about it as a concept.

Opening your heart involves breaking old habits born out of fear and illusion and transforming them into new practices of radical self-honoring and loving-kindness. Move toward repeatedly sending loving-kindness to yourself so that with each breath your heart pumps compassion, self-acceptance, and love through every molecule in your being.

Lesson Seven Resources

Gifts

- Opening your heart starts first with compassion and respect toward yourself.

- Your heart is not a fragile, delicate bird, but a resilient, powerful hawk learning to fly.

- Unconditional love does not mean you are always happy or perfect. It means you lovingly accept your mistakes, flaws, and fears.

- Learning to send loving-kindness to everyone, regardless of their actions, releases your spirit to soar.

Explorations

Heart Opening Practice

Spend some time massaging your breasts and feeling them as an extension of your heart. Feel the muscles around your chest and bring healing touch to any armoring. Massage your arms and hands, and imagine opening up your hands so more energy can pour down into everything you touch. Massage out with love all the old agreements that keep your heart chakra closed. Sometimes touch can help us unlock the hidden agreements. You may want to speak out loud what you are releasing. Then use your gentle touch to massage in healing and aliveness.

Now consciously practice standing up straight, breasts out, heart open as you interact in the world. Notice when you want to contract or slouch. Notice the difference in your being energetically when you collapse your chest versus when you consciously open it.

What Feeds Your Heart?

When you are making a decision, ask yourself, does this nourish my heart? What shift do I need to make so my heart feels fed? Get beyond your stories of what you want and listen to your heart, not your mind! You will need to get quiet and listen in a new way. There may still be fear and difficult choices, but your heart's voice will ring sweetly.

Speak Your Truth

*Do you really want to look back on your
life and see how wonderful it could have
been had you not been afraid to live it?*

—Caroline Myss

Linda is an accomplished psychiatrist, athlete, mother, and all-around Warrior Goddess woman. I had known her for years and been coaching her for about six months when I discovered something hardly anyone knew about her: In many of her personal relationships, she was terrified of speaking her truth, or using her voice to outwardly express emotion. Despite the fact that Linda spent hours every day using her voice to share insights and information with her therapy clients, she couldn't bring herself to tell people how she really felt about situations that were upsetting to her, preferring instead to keep quiet and not "rock the boat." I prescribed an exercise to help her break this pattern. I asked her to put on loud music, dance around the house, and let herself be vocal in any way she wanted to. At this suggestion, she froze and stated quietly, "I can't do that!"

"What can you do?" I asked her. Linda started by singing aloud one word of a song while in the car. She said even that simple outward expression caused her whole body to shake. She gradually trained herself to move past her huge discomfort until she could sing an entire song. Then I encouraged her to start talking to herself out loud while she was at home. Eventually she graduated to expressing emotion verbally. She told me this was one of the hardest things she had ever done, and that it took a lot of courage to keep breaking through the old patterning she learned as a child around being silent.

It is surprising how many successful and otherwise outspoken women have trouble speaking their truth in the situations that matter most. We use our voices all the time, but many of us were never taught how to use our words to communicate or stand up for ourselves in difficult or awkward circumstances.

Most of us are not taught good communication skills; gossip, judgment, and defensiveness are all too prevalent growing up. And as girls we often are also supposed to be ladylike and sweet, especially as children and sometimes beyond.

Repeat these phrases to yourself: "Don't speak unless spoken to." "Be seen but not heard." "Don't say anything to upset others." Notice how you feel inside when you say these words in your head. For many of us, lessons learned in childhood taught us to close down our true, authentic voice. Often by the time we are adults we have no idea how we actually feel or think about things, let alone how to convey that information clearly to others!

Authentic communication does not have clauses on it from the mind, such as "I must be kind so I do not hurt others' feelings." Look more deeply at these types of self-monitoring thoughts. Why must you be kind so you do not hurt others' feelings? When you answer honestly, you will probably find it is because you are uncomfortable standing in the face of someone's hurt or disappointment or anger. You are being kind not because it is in alignment with your deepest truth, but as a way to avoid others' reactions.

The more authentic you become in being and expressing who you really are, the more love, presence, and kindness arise spontaneously within you. You won't have to try to be kind to others; you will just be kind because it is your nature. This is not about being one way or another. It is about being willing to be honest, which is a kindness to yourself that will then spill over to others.

Keep exploring what you specifically want to communicate, and why. When you release the old rules of who you are supposed to be, which are often preceded by the words *should,* *have to,* or *must,* you create the space to stop trying to be your best so you can just be your best.

When you first start speaking your truth, it can feel awkward, wrong, and scary. It does not feel like you are saving energy, but losing it! This is the initial resistance of your belief system. Do not expect to feel great when you first speak up. Give yourself time to stalk and clear out the emotions and beliefs that arise. Notice, without judgment: Was I able to keep my heart open? How do I feel about myself now? Did I say exactly what I meant to?

When you do not speak your truth and either hold it inside or placate others, you often end up creating resentments against others and yourself. You get mad at yourself for not speaking your mind, or mad at others for not understanding how you really feel (forgetting that you never told them how you feel!). In organizations and family systems, this creates distrust, gossip, and fear, and what is commonly referred to as "drama." When these resentments toward others build up, we sometimes explode in a venting of emotions and judgment in an unconscious or punishing manner. When this occurs, you are not speaking from a place of love, but rather from your wounds and hurt, often not realizing your part in the situation, which was that you did not communicate how you really felt in the first place. Intimate relationships then become hollow and dissatisfying, and your own trust of self is diminished each time you do not speak what you really mean.

To speak from your integrity, you need to identify and root out the old beliefs about communication you learned growing up or picked up from your culture and made your own. I have listed some common societal beliefs below. Take a moment to reflect on whether or not they are true for you.

Growing up, I was taught or believed:	True	False
Children and/or girls should be seen and not heard.		
Lie to someone if you think the truth will hurt them.		
Women who "speak their mind" are bossy.		
Women should support whatever their partner prefers.		
Women should put the needs of others ahead of their own.		
Women should be demure and quiet.		
Girls shouldn't like loud things.		
It is better to not say anything than to upset others.		

You may need to start taking very little baby steps around speaking your truth. Start with things like asking people for the time with your heart open. Or take one day and say no to anything anyone asks you. (Perhaps not at work, though—unless this is the best place for you to practice!) Speak the truth to yourself. Are you scared? Excited? Nervous? Do you like this person? Do you want to eat Mexican or Italian? You may have to dig to find out what your preferences are if you have stayed silent and let others make decisions for you. Find where you are afraid of making boundaries, and experiment. Be bold and practice, practice, practice, not closing down.

At the same time, remember to be gentle with yourself. Learning to speak your truth is a lifelong relationship. I still work to be authentic in my communication. My two main strategies are pleaser and controller, so I consciously ask myself: Did I really say what I meant to say? Was I saying that to try to get a specific outcome?

I don't believe we ever "master" the art of learning to communicate effectively. But we do get more skilled at witnessing ourselves and making new choices.

The fastest way to create discomfort and resentment in your life is to say yes when you mean no. If someone asks you to do something, and you say yes out of a feeling of obligation, or because you don't want to hurt the other person's feelings, then you are not speaking your truth in that situation. Being your true, authentic, Warrior Goddess self means you can say no from a place of love rather than say yes from a place of fear.

One note of caution: Speaking your truth does not mean you always say everything you are thinking. As with the previous steps on the path, being a Warrior Goddess requires discernment. We must be careful not to use the practice of speaking our truth as an excuse to be cruel or hurtful. Simply put, the spirit of this practice means you are willing to delve deeper into your own truth and your own inner guidance, and you are willing to speak this truth even in situations where your listener may be uncomfortable with what you have to say.

To find and maintain this balance, we must evaluate and unweave any old agreements that we have around verbal communication. Remember that your destination is to experience openhearted, fluid communication and vibrant expression, using your inner knowing as a guide. As coach and author Martha Beck says, "No matter how difficult and painful it may be, nothing sounds as good to the soul as the truth."

Owning Your Words

One of my favorite books on communication is *Messages: The Communication Skills Book* by Matthew McKay, Martha Davis, and Patrick Fanning. It is a great guide for cleaning up what the authors call "contaminated" or "partial" messages.

A contaminated message is when your energy does not match your words. "I see you are late again," can be said cleanly, as an observation. Or the same words can be a vehicle for sarcasm, bitterness, blame, or frustration. "I see you are late again," said with clenched body and an angry tone, is a contaminated message because you are putting your frustrated and hurt energy into a simple statement of fact. When you are learning to be clear with your words, it is vital that you become clear with the energy you put behind them. The practice of speaking your truth isn't just about the words you use, but also carries the responsibility that your speech is free of contaminated messages, or words that are loaded with negative feelings.

A partial message doesn't convey the full range of deep communication. McKay invites us to share whole messages when we are in an intimate conversation. Whole messages include our observation of the situation (the facts), our thoughts (which may be true or not true), our feelings (our emotional experience), and our needs (what do we want?). Separating these four different aspects of communication is a great education in where we hold back or distort our voice.

A fact is the observable, measurable, honest-to-goodness truth of what happened. When I initially started naming the facts of a situation first, I found it was surprisingly challenging! We tend to lead with statements such as "you always" or "you never" when we are upset. Stating the facts of the situation invites us to slow down, step back, and see what is really going on. Here is the difference: "You are always late!" to "The last two times we met you were a half hour late and didn't call me." The observation is just that: neutral, without story or emotion. It may take awhile to track what the facts are, especially when we are really upset by someone else's actions.

Our thoughts are the words running around in our head about the situation. Our thoughts are not necessarily the truth; they are just what we are thinking in the moment. They are also not our emotions, so we want to keep our emotions and our thoughts separate. "I wonder if you were scared, and I felt hurt and abandoned by your actions" is much clearer than "You wanted to hurt me and your messed-up childhood is ruining my life." We get to become more intimate with our thoughts when we practice clear communication.

And we also get to be more honest and intimate with what our emotional responses are. The third part of clear communication is sharing our feelings. Since we often share our stories and not our vulnerable feelings, this can sometimes feel scary. Keep asking yourself, "How did this situation make me feel?" Avoid telling others that they made you feel any particular way. They didn't make you feel—no one can actually make you feel anything, because no one is inside of you creating the emotional reaction but you. Shift from "You made me feel" to "I felt." Be mindful of how easy it is to blame others for your state of mind: "I felt that you abandoned me" is actually not accurate, because you are giving the other person power over your emotions, which only you have. Take the other out of your feeling statements, so they are about you: Say "I felt X" rather than "I felt you made me X." "I felt betrayed and shocked" takes your power back, and communicates with the other person what happened inside of you.

The fourth part of clear communication, stating your needs, can sometimes really throw you for a loop! As I learned to communicate more clearly, I was surprised to find that I had the facts, could name my thoughts, and felt my feelings, but I had no idea what I wanted. It was tremendously empowering to name the need. "I'd like it if you picked up your clothes off the floor and put them in the hamper." "Please call me if you are going to be more than ten minutes late." "I need more structure: Can we set up a time to create an outline for the project?"

Important note: Just because you share a need doesn't mean the person you are talking to can fulfill it, or even that they should! What is most important is being clear with what your need is, then exploring how to fulfill that need in creative ways with yourself or with others. Be clear about what you want, and find out if you can speak about it and make conscious agreements.

What I've found in being more conscious in communication is the importance of bringing in humor, clarity, and both ears to all conversations.

Speaking Your Truth

I'd like to share with you the following example of speaking your truth that occurred with a woman I coached. Wendy had been in a relationship with her girlfriend Sue for many years.

On the whole, their relationship was a healthy one, but Wendy noticed that in certain stressful situations she was afraid to speak her truth, and instead would shut down. This occurred in situations when Sue would raise her voice.

Once on the Warrior Goddess path, Wendy took the following actions. First, she waited to talk about the situation until they were both in a good space. When both people are frustrated and upset it is no use talking, because there is no one there to listen. So her first action was to wait for the emotions to dissipate. The next day, she sat down with Sue and said, "Honey, last night when we were talking about finances you raised your voice and it scares me when you raise your voice. When you do that, my reason shuts down and I pull away because I am afraid you will hurt me. I know you will never hurt me, but I still have this response in my body. I would like to ask that if you are upset at me that we take some time out to cool down, and then we talk. That way I'll be able to stay more present with you and really hear what you are saying."

Her next action was to really listen to Sue's response. Listening beneath people's words and asking clarifying questions creates more intimacy. Listening is the power twin to speaking. In this case, Sue saw that raising her voice was her own defense mechanism based on old agreements and that it was triggering unwanted effects in her relationship with Wendy. Consequently, she made a commitment to work on remaining calm. So far, this conscious and open communication has been wonderful for their relationship.

Now, let's say you're in a similar situation and your partner says, "OK, I will stop raising my voice" but then continues to yell when he or she gets frustrated. If this happens, it's tempting to feel betrayed or angry and either shut down or begin yelling back. But the Warrior Goddess path invites you to not take the bait, thereby falling into your own unconscious reaction, but rather to simply make a note to yourself: "OK, they are still raising their voice."

You have a choice in what you do next. You can retreat consciously, remembering that your partner is trying to break an old behavioral pattern too, and return to the conversation when things have calmed down.

Another option is to give your partner some space to relearn and make new choices by bringing awareness with humor to the conversation. Perhaps you tickle them and say, "Hey, remember, no yelling! Let's run around the house together and then talk!" You can create a game with each other and make fun agreements, like when the conversation gets heated you both have to jump rope for three minutes before you talk. Or the person who is upset has to wear a funny hat. Sometimes silliness is the antidote for getting back to in-the-present communication. Breaking the pattern by doing something different can work wonders.

The one thing I want to make clear in this example is that judging someone for not following through with their own agreement is a waste of your precious energy. When someone breaks an agreement, going into blame and judgment and betrayal does not help. But getting clear again about what you need and how you can fulfill that need is vital.

"The next time you yell, I will leave the room and wait until you are calm. I simply need the space to stay grounded, and I cannot do that when I feel attacked." Can you say this with warrior clarity and a goddess's open heart? If your heart is closed, you are judging the person or yourself. Try speaking from an open place. This is where change happens. At first it may seem that this escalates the problem. But if you stay clear with your boundaries and follow through, a shift will occur.

The Heart-Throat Connection

Coming from your heart is vital when learning to speak your truth. If we don't really mean what we say, it won't matter how well we say it; the people we are speaking to will feel the lack of sincerity behind the words. It is powerful to dedicate yourself to speaking your truth with your heart open, even if that truth is difficult, rather than trying to be gentle or appropriate and speak with your heart closed.

One way we close our heart and throat is when we believe we are doing something wrong. So, again, looking deeply into our unconscious beliefs is crucial. Is it OK for you to say no? Is it OK for you to make boundaries? Is it OK for you to say things others may not want to hear? Can you speak without taking responsibility for others' reactions? And can you do all of these things with your heart wide open? This takes practice. Speaking your truth is often not something we are supported to do, but it is a skill we can learn to do gracefully.

If you fail to speak your truth, your internal energy will then either build up and eventually explode in an emotional outburst, or your energetic flow will be cut off and you will feel like your access to pure life-force energy has dried up, leaving you feeling lethargic and without passion, timidly saying what you think others want to hear and needing others as a source of energy and direction. When you deny your own voice, this feeds your judge or victim voices, rather than your authenticity, and the result is anger at yourself or others.

Finding Your Authentic Voice

Two very helpful tools when working on finding your authentic voice are backtracking and replaying.

Backtracking

Backtracking means you make an internal commitment to speaking your truth in the moment, and if you do not, you go back to the person, admit you did not speak your truth, and try again. You may have to backtrack over and over again until you get it right.

Here is an example. A friend asks you, "Do you want to go to a movie with me tomorrow night?" And you automatically say yes. But after you get off the phone you realize you really want to stay home and read a book. So instead of going to the movie, you call back and say, "I realized after I got off the phone that I do not want to go to a movie tomorrow, I need to rest. Can we go to the movie next week?" You do not need to explain yourself or apologize profusely; simply state what you need. Watch out for defending yourself.

The great thing about committing to this practice is that after we backtrack a few times we learn really quickly to speak honestly in the moment.

Replaying

With replaying, you consciously replay conversations from your past when you didn't speak your truth, but this time, you imagine yourself speaking your truth. There are probably plenty of situations you can think of where you realize that you did not speak your truth in the moment. What would speaking your truth have looked like? Replay the situation using your authentic voice. What would you have said differently, and how would it have potentially changed the outcome?

I was once in a relationship with a man who felt threatened by the way I was dressing and being in the world. We had long, teary talks about my not being overtly sexual. He was in a place of wanting to have a stable, monogamous relationship.

At the time I was just beginning to explore my sexuality, and if I had been honest with myself and with him I would have said, "Sweetie, I care a lot about you and really want to be in a relationship with you, but right now I need to play and flirt and explore being sexy." He may have said, "OK, I can hold with that as long as we keep these agreements," and we may have negotiated, or he may have said, "I cannot do that." Instead, we spent three tumultuous years in a relationship where I repressed my sexual energy (you can imagine what that did for our sex life!) and he felt cut off.

We were in different places in our needs, but both of us ignored the truth of this. Looking back, I see how powerful it would have been to speak my truth and not be ashamed of it or cling to being in a relationship with him in the way he wanted to be in a relationship.

It is a gift to yourself and others when you are truly, open-heartedly honest. This starts with speaking the truth to yourself first, over and over and over again. In doing so you will gain self-intimacy and trust, which will naturally spill over into all of your relationships.

Lesson Eight Resources

Gifts

- Clear communication often means unlearning bad habits, and sometimes we need to go back to "first grade" basics.
- Speaking our truth is often as uncomfortable as it is empowering.
- Learn to communicate in whole messages to increase intimacy and connection.

- An open heart is a powerful ally, even when we are making boundaries or sharing difficult information.

Explorations

Finding Your Truth

To learn more about your own truth in communicating, write down everything you believe about how you should communicate in the world. Write without thinking. Read the list over and notice which agreements/thoughts are about getting a desired result/reaction from the person you are talking to, and which stem from your authentic expression.

Vent, Advice, Share

My friend and I play a simple game that helps us stay present with each other. If one of us needs to vent and express our frustration after a hard day, we say, "Vent!" The other person can say, "Give it to me!" One person takes five minutes to vent as fully and dramatically as possible, and once those five minutes are up you stop and move on. We can also say, "Not now!" which means "I don't have the space for your vent right now."

If we need advice, we say, "Advice!" so that the other knows to get their creative brain in gear.

And if we say "Share!" that means "I'm really excited about something—cheerlead and celebrate with me!"

What games could you create with friends, family, or partners?

Embody Your Wisdom

The intuitive mind is a sacred gift and the rational mind is a faithful servant. We have created a society that honors the servant and has forgotten the gift.

—Albert Einstein

I was running late for an appointment when I felt the strong urge to visit my neighbor. My rational mind said, "You need to get going, there is no reason to visit Fred." But something deeper in my being kept saying, "Just walk next door, see how he is doing." After I argued with myself for a while, I decided to follow the pull to see my neighbor. As I walked down the little dirt path and through the oak trees, I called my client and said I was going to be a little bit late.

Fred had been going through some really difficult circumstances: the end of his marriage, the possibility of having to leave the home he loved, his young son being miles away. When I walked up he looked up from cooking dinner, surprised to see me.

"What are you doing here?" he asked.

"I just felt the urge to come see you," I said as I plopped down into a chair. "How are you?"

He sat silent for a long time. "Well," he said, "I was actually just cooking my last meal. I have decided to end my life."

I got really quiet inside, and opened my heart to him and to what he needed to hear. "That seems a little drastic," I said.

Fred laughed. "I just don't feel I can do it any longer."

"I understand. You are going through a lot. But I think life is worth living, and you still have so much to offer the world." We spent the next half hour together, with me mostly listening and staying present with him in my body, heart, and mind. I let go of any agenda and trusted that I was brought here for a reason.

"I can't believe you came by," Fred told me after he shared his fears and anguish. "You are right, I don't want to end it all. If you hadn't come by I would have shot myself tonight. Thanks for being my angel."

As I walked back to my house I said a prayer of thanks that I had slowed down enough to listen and follow my inner guidance.

Here's another story. A few years ago, a dear friend of mine was on her way home from the store on a Sunday afternoon when she had a strong feeling she should go and see her father. It was a typical south Texas summer day, with temperatures hovering around 100 degrees, and her first thought was to dismiss the notion of an unplanned visit and head home for a much-needed dip in the pool.

But the feeling wouldn't go away, and instead grew stronger and stronger until she couldn't ignore it any longer. Turning her car around, she drove twenty minutes to his house, where he now lived alone after the death of her mother five years previously.

She opened the front door and announced as she entered, "Daddy, it's me!" But instead of hearing a reply she was met with silence. She quickly glanced through all the rooms but couldn't find her father anywhere. His car was out front, and since he was creature of habit, she knew he rarely went anywhere on Sunday after church.

Then she noticed that the sliding glass door to the backyard was unlocked. She hurried outside to find her father facedown in the grass, the blistering summer sun pounding down on him. She turned him over, and though he was clearly pale and dehydrated, he was still breathing. She dialed 911, and within a few minutes they were on the way to the emergency room via ambulance, where the doctors confirmed her father had had a heart attack. They said if she had arrived any later he would not have survived. Without a doubt, her intuition saved his life.

I have never met a woman who hasn't experienced the power of intuition in some form or another. From the small matters like when you think of an old friend you haven't spoken with in years moments before they call, or the larger episodes like the two I just recounted, intuition is a potent force in the Universe.

Our intuition is proof that there is more to life than what can be weighed, measured, or otherwise quantified in a lab. The laws of science cannot explain intuition, yet we all know it's real based on our personal experience. By definition, intuition is from the realm of the spiritual.

Closely related to intuition is the concept of wisdom. This is not the type of wisdom that can be gained from reading a book; rather, it is more like a deep sense of knowing, a feeling that comes from your heart. When you think and act from this seat of wisdom, you move along the path of life, tapping into the strength to deal with whatever may come your way. A Warrior Goddess speaks, acts, and engages from this place of wisdom, or what the Toltec call "silent knowledge."

Listening to your intuition and being in your wisdom are vital skills of a Warrior Goddess, and they stem from our ability to get still, connect, and listen beneath our rational understanding.

There is a reason this is the ninth Warrior Goddess lesson, and that is because when you practice the prior lessons, walking in your wisdom and listening to your intuition become much, much easier. In fact, doing these things becomes a way of life.

As the two stories at the beginning of this chapter illustrate, being in touch with your intuition is a powerful tool as you move through the world. It's one way you can connect directly with the spiritual realm and tap into that unseen power of the Universe, receiving guidance on matters as big as life and death and as small as where to park your car in the lot.

When we are out of touch with our intuition, we often get fixated on the world of physical forms, and as a result our lives either grow dull or very stressful, or we get consumed by wanting to succeed on the physical plane. We become slaves to physical things that we think will make us feel better, such as shopping, eating, drinking, or abusing drugs and alcohol. Instead of trusting ourselves, we turn to sexual connections to feel safe. Rather than moving in harmony with the way the world is, we attempt to use our will to force things to happen the way we think they should. This is not the path of the Warrior Goddess.

When we are out of balance with our lives in this way, we may end up hearing the voice of fear and mistaking it for our intuition, or we may give up on our intuition entirely, instead relying on others to be the voice of divine guidance in our life.

With care, we can develop and nourish our innate spiritual knowing. We can reopen our intuitive and spiritual centers, no matter how long they have been closed or hidden.

Distinguishing the Mind's Habits from True Intuition

How do you know which messages are coming from your intuition and which are coming from your mind? That's a question every Warrior Goddess should ask as she develops her intuition.

Using our intuitive birthright is about learning to trust more than our historical knowing. Intuition comes from a place of love, not fear. The voice of your mind can be very tricky and masquerade as intuition, but you will get better at recognizing the differences between the two over time. Remember that with intuition you are often looking for a *feeling* rather than a *thought*. Many women describe it as the classic "gut" feeling that originates in the solar plexus, while others feel a flash of energy throughout the body. Some women have pictures or images appear in their minds, or hear a sound or notice a smell that brings information. As you begin to know yourself and your intuitive signs better, you will be more cognitive of the signs that appear to you.

The mind is the sum total of your experiences and belief systems, and it often operates from a place of fear and desire. "I want this. I don't want that" are thoughts that the mind manufactures. This does not mean the mind is "bad," but it's important to be aware of these habits and see how the mind's desires and fears can masquerade as intuition. The skill of the Warrior Goddess is to distinguish the habits of the mind from genuine intuitive messages. The first step is to untangle intuition and spiritual connection from any of your old stories and belief systems. I've watched myself and many others have strong "intuitive" feelings about something only to discover upon further investigation that the feelings are not actually intuition, but the mind talking.

My first wake-up call around confusing intuition with story came around the end of a relationship after I graduated from college. Ted and I had a fast and intense courtship and relationship, filled with long, dreamy days spent looking into each other's eyes and that giddy happiness of new love. We also had a very strong bond around both of us healing from sexual abuse. Unfortunately, our genuine care for each other was soon tangled with our unconscious fears and wounds, and we parted when Ted decided he needed to go to New Mexico to find himself.

When he returned unexpectedly I found that even though we said we didn't want to be in relationship anymore, I kept being connected to him through a series of undeniable synchronicities. I'd think about him and decide to go by his old house, and I'd find him outside. I'd feel the urge to go for a walk late at night and run into him. We would have passionate sex, and then we wouldn't see each other until the next synchronicity brought us together. I felt it was fate; obviously we were meant to be together. I believed I was following my intuition, and I wove a whole story of the undying passion of our love.

A few months later, a woman in the community I lived in came into my office and told me she and Ted were in a relationship. She had given him an ultimatum to tell me by a certain date, and since he hadn't she wanted to make sure I knew.

It took me weeks to sort out why my intuition had led me astray. How could I be getting so many messages from the Universe that Ted was the right one for me? As I investigated, I started to see the many things I had overlooked, all the little signs that pointed to the truth. My "intuitive hits" were actually my unhealthy connection to someone who was not available. This experience was invaluable in helping me find the subtle differences between true intuition and acting from past wounding or fears.

This is why it is very important to take the time to work all the lessons in Warrior Goddess Training, so you learn about your belief structures and the ways in which you have held yourself back in the past. As you systematically clean up the different areas in your life, your intuitive wisdom becomes much clearer, like a mirror after a good polishing.

Exercise: Watching the Outcome

Building your own intuitive abilities takes a willingness to be wrong and a willingness to be right. We learn in hindsight what the language of our innate intuition is. I've found the best way is to "watch the outcome" with great curiosity and learn the subtleties of an intuitive sign versus one from the mind.

"Watch the outcome" works like this: When you have what you believe to be an intuitive feeling or response, mark what the feeling is like. Where did you sense it in your body? What did the voice sound like in your head? How do you feel emotionally? What happened with your energy body? Track all the different aspects of what you perceive to be your intuition. Make a conscious decision to follow it or not follow it.

I recommend creating an intuition journal and writing down all the insights/experiences you have that you think might be intuition. Then later watch and see what the outcome is. In hindsight, ask yourself, was that message from your intuition or your mind? How did following the message or not following it unfold? By writing things down and then watching the outcome, you will begin to recognize where you were clear and where you were off target. Over time you will find that you get much better in your ability to identify which feelings are likely intuitive and which ones are not.

Here are a few examples of watching the outcome and tracking your intuition versus your mind's habits:

Date: 2/12/13

Feeling/thought: I need to leave for work early today.

Action: I left for work ten minutes early.

Details: My voice was quiet, and I felt calm. I wanted to stay in bed longer, so part of me wanted to ignore the thought that I needed to leave early. But in the end I decided to get up and get out the door.

Result: I walked into the office and the phone was ringing. It was someone I'd been needing to talk to about our project. Happy dance!

What I learned: Follow the quiet voice, even when my body-mind doesn't want to.

Date: 5/6/13

Feeling/thought: I was at work and I felt I needed to go to the store right away, that it was really important.

Action: I grabbed my coat and headed out.

Details: On the way to the store I felt better, so I decided I was making the right decision. I shopped for groceries and then decided to also pick up a few things at the nursery.

Result: I got totally busy with other things when I got home and had to put the plants away. Then I started weeding.

What I learned: It's a couple of weeks later and I've been seeing this pattern pop up all over the place: a need to do something immediately that feels like strong intuition. But I'm seeing now that it is just a distraction from work, and it causes me to be stressed out in the long run even though I feel better in the short run. When I asked myself, "Is this feeling my intuition or a distraction?" and sat with the urgency of the feeling, I realized that what was beneath it was the thought "I can't do this task—it is too hard."

New action: The next time I suspect that I might be getting some false intuition, I'm going to take a short break and walk around to release energy. As I'm walking, I'll give myself a pep talk on how wonderfully competent and talented I am at my job.

When you are watching the outcome it is important to not judge yourself! Remember, you are learning. Be curious and patient about the subtle differences between an intuitive knowing and a mind story. As you can tease apart the threads of old habits and fears and reweave your life from the stronger weaving of inner knowing, you will open to the fountain of sacred wisdom that flows within you.

I've found that for many women, intuitive knowing is strong, but our capacity to trust ourselves is weak. My friend Sally tells a story about a time she didn't listen to her intuition. Despite a gut knowing that a situation wasn't right for her, she kept denying her intuition until she became physically sick. It was only when she stopped to really listen to what was true for her, and was willing to see it, that she understood that by ignoring her intuition she was creating a great imbalance within herself.

Here are a few other things to explore as you deepen your relationship with your intuition and learn to trust its true voice.

Know What Your Filters Are

Sometimes your initial intuitive sense is clear, but then you filter the message through your opinions and experiences, and the desires and fears of the mind take over. As a result, you cloud the original truth that came to you via your intuition.

Use Others' Intuitive Insights with Care

Another difficulty you may have is distinguishing between your intuition and other people's opinions (or your mind's projections of what their opinions are!). In other words, if you have an intuitive moment where you feel compelled to take a specific action, you may immediately hear the voice of someone you know speaking in your head saying, "Don't do that!" or "It will never work!" In this way, you filter the intuitive sign through the beliefs and opinions of others.

Also along these lines, we can have friends with strong intuition, or we may seek out the services of a professional psychic (*intuition* is the mainstream word for "psychic phenomenon"). In either case, we need to be aware that others, like ourselves, may have strong filters or belief systems that can cloud their interpretation of the information they receive. So although the initial information may be accurate, it may be contaminated by their belief system. Be sure to validate the information yourself, and stay aware of the belief systems of anyone you seek advice from.

For example, a woman may give you intuitive advice about your marriage, but her "knowing" about relationships could be twisted by anger at her ex-husband. Knowing this is huge. Use others as a resource to tap into your own intuitive knowing, rather than as the absolute truth. Walking the Warrior Goddess path means learning to keep the emotions and thoughts of others separate from what is true for you. You can still respect the opinions of others without necessarily having to agree with them.

Know When to Act

Lastly, recognize that just because you intuit something does not mean an action needs to be taken. For example, I remember sitting with an apprentice and feeling into the energy of the choices she was making at the time. My intuitional vision was very clear, and I could see down the pathway of her choices, and the challenging outcome she was going to have to face in the near future. At the time I felt really frustrated, but I also knew her mind was made up and that she needed to have these experiences for herself. As a result, I knew the best thing for me to do was to stay silent. And then, as event after event unfolded as I intuited it would, the true benefit was in her learning the lesson she needed to for herself. I was grateful I'd used my intuiting of what was coming for her not as a way to be superior or right, but to help me stay compassionate toward her and unconditionally support her in benefiting from her experiences.

Wisdom and Silent Knowledge

In tribal cultures around the world the elders are important decision makers and holders of wisdom. The grandmothers or female elders were honored and sought after to counsel on matters big and small. These women were the third vital part of an ancient female archetypical trinity: maiden, mother, and crone.

The maiden is the energy of curiosity, exploration, youth, innocence, play, and sexual and sensual expression. The mother archetype is the energy of birthing and nourishing, whether this is children or projects of the heart. The crone archetype is the energy of sustainable, long-term, beneficial actions, nourishing the entire tribe without discrimination, and visionary wisdom. When we embrace our crone we embody the best qualities of the maiden and mother and are in service to the highest good for all.

Balanced Warrior Goddesses contain all three aspects of this divine feminine trinity, blending the best qualities of the maiden, mother, and crone.

It is interesting to me that modern society is so fixated on the maiden end of the spectrum. That seems so unbalanced. Just check out any magazine and you'll see this imbalance reflected clearly. Imagine if all mainstream magazines were filled with images of happy crones and powerful elders! While the maiden energy is wonderful and important, when we strive to remain maidens past that stage we can cut off our power and depth. It is much too easy to get caught in the hamster wheel of trying to retain our youth at all costs. I'm not talking about taking good care of ourselves and staying young at heart. I'm talking about those times when we might look in the mirror and judge ourselves for our wrinkles, or the shape of our breasts, or the other changes that have happened since were twenty years old.

We are also out of balance with the mother aspect of our inner trinity. The mother archetype is a powerful one, but many of us end up feeling undervalued, overstressed, and drained by the mother aspect of the feminine because we have learned to mother everything at the expense of ourselves. We also can hold on to the mother archetype long after it serves us or our children, (s)mothering them even after they are grown and on their own.

To change this pattern, I invite all of us Warrior Goddess women to step up and make friends with the power of the crone. This means going beyond our fear of our power, letting go of trying to be nonthreatening little girls or enticing sexpots, and releasing the habit of putting everyone else first without including our needs. It's time we claim our innate crone wisdom.

When we fearlessly step toward the crone energy, we access our Toltec "silent knowledge." Silent knowledge includes but transcends our intuition. When we are connected to our intuition, we are receiving messages from the invisible world of spirit that helps us navigate this material world of form. When we connect with silent knowledge, we erase the boundary between these two worlds of spirit and matter, known and unknown. We step beyond duality, beyond right and wrong, beyond rules and into absolute connection with all that is.

As don Miguel writes, "Inner silence is the place of silent knowledge where you know everything, and you can see that there are multiple choices."

We all were born connected to silent knowledge, and at any time we can reconnect to this birthright. Silent knowledge arises when we become still and expand our perception beyond our ego and personality and into the always-present truth that we are one with all of life. We unplug from our own self-importance and realize that we are each a tiny cell in the body of the Universe. From this awareness we don't need to look for answers; answers arise spontaneously within us because we are everything.

The first step in developing a clear link to silent knowledge is to simply intend one. Your intent is powerful. You can stay narrowly focused on your small pasture of day-to-day drama and fears, or jump the fence and head for the unknown.

Open beyond your knowing to the awareness that all things are one and interconnected. Slow down. Listen to the stars and the soil; hear the silent teachings of the wind and the wisdom of fire. The microcosm of each of your cells is a direct link to the macrocosm of the entire Universe. Get still and let the Universe blossom within you.

Lesson Nine Resources

Gifts

- Your intuition is always talking; your work is to remember how to listen to that inner voice.

- Strong intuitive knowings don't necessarily need to be expressed, understood, or followed.

- Energetic perception comes in myriad forms: through an inner knowing, through seeing, and through feeling.

- The wisdom of silent knowledge comes when we quiet our mind and focus on the unknown rather than the known.

Explorations

Deepen Your Silence

Now that you are firmly planted on the Warrior Goddess path, it's time to raise your commitment to your spiritual practices. The following exercises will help you be more in touch with your intuition and wisdom.

- Take one hour to be in silence once a week.

- Practice partial silence at a party or at work: Limit your speaking to only what is necessary. Fill the spaces between with love or a specific intent.

- Several times a day, stop multitasking. When you are eating, just eat. When you are talking on the phone, just talk.

- Create more spaciousness in each moment through your conscious breath and intent. Even when you are really busy, you can slow yourself down and feel into the silence between seconds.

- Plan a time for an extended silence. Get clear on what you will need to do to make this happen. Ask for support. Create guidelines for yourself.

- Make agreements and clear boundaries with children, partners, and friends around when you will be in silence.

- If you usually are silent in the world, do just the opposite! Run experiments to talk more and express yourself in the world. Look at what will challenge you the most.

Choose Your Path

Life shrinks or expands in proportion to one's courage.

—Anaïs Nin

We were about five minutes into a workshop I was teaching when a woman raised her hand and said, "I don't know if I should be here. I am an introvert, and you are very extroverted and the energy here feels too big for me. I might have to leave." I told her, "I'm actually an introvert too who does well as an extrovert when I am teaching. You are welcome to leave if that is what you need to do, but I invite you to stay and see what is here for you. I'm not asking you to be different, I'm inviting you to stretch and open to new possibilities."

She did stay for the entire workshop, and at the end of the day she excitedly shared, "I had no idea how much my story about being an introvert was limiting me!" She was glowing with newfound freedom.

Now, does this mean that she will go on to become an extrovert who loves being in big groups? Probably not (unless that is who she really is!). I share this story to show that stepping into your Warrior Goddess power means letting go of who you have been before so you can experience who you are once you are freed from old definitions and perceptions.

I used to consider myself an incredibly shy person. One day, I was asked to stand in for someone and talk about something I was really passionate about—a recent journey I'd been on to Nicaragua to bring toys and medicine to children. Even though I was terrified, I found that once I opened my mouth I loved sharing. It was a revelation. How could I be so shy and have just enjoyed being in front of two hundred people? I had to let go of who I thought I was and the familiar role I had taken on as a shy person in order to let in the truth: I love teaching in front of groups. I still get shy at times, but now my world is much bigger than my old definition of myself as a shy introvert. Now I see myself as someone who is blessed to be rooted in stillness and overflowing with words and energy.

As we approach the end of this book, I invite you to remember that there is no one way to be a Warrior Goddess. You may be a loud, outgoing, talkative Warrior Goddess, or you may be a quiet, introverted Warrior Goddess who prefers to watch a crowd rather than join or lead one. Or you may be both! The key is, once you are on the Warrior Goddess path, you realize you have a choice. You are no longer a slave to other people's ideas about how you should live your life, nor are you trapped by your own outdated belief system. You are becoming the woman you *want* to be, which is synonymous with who you are *meant* to be.

So the final lesson of this book is about joyfully choosing how to define yourself as you continue along the path.

Choosing how you define yourself is not an exercise in limiting yourself, nor is it designed to foster a false sense of importance. Choosing how to define yourself as you go forward on the path is a way to create positive direction and continue inner healing. But remember, there is danger in extremes: Avoid creating a rigid definition of who you should be and then using it to beat yourself up for not being it, or having no direction and wandering without purpose, making choices by default.

In the next section we'll explore the most familiar roles that we use to define and often limit ourselves, and how to consciously choose new myths that expand and inspire us.

Roles

A role is a script written long before we were born. A role defines how you should act, how you should respond, and what you should believe. We often take on a role without recognizing it is a role, and then suddenly we find ourselves acting in ways we don't understand or don't like. When we identify with a role we believe it is who we are, not just a part we are playing.

Daughter, mother, student, addict, teacher, boss, girlfriend, volunteer, artist, activist, healer, the happy one, the sad one, single, divorced, the caretaker, the spiritual one, victim, perpetrator, good worker, widow . . . these are all possible roles we could have adopted over the years. And there are many, many others.

What different roles have you held over your lifetime? List as many as you can. Notice how each of these labels feels in your body.

Any role we have an attachment to needs to be released with love. An integrated Warrior Goddess does not need to lean on any roles to feel whole (including the role of Warrior Goddess!). And unweaving yourself from the roles you have taken on may take time. Be patient and be honest. Where do you still energetically hold on to outside support and validation? The exercise below will help you start brainstorming the roles you carry, both consciously and unconsciously, and see the places where they constrict you.

Exercise: Identifying Your Roles

In this exercise, you're going to define your roles and come up with a plan to change or maintain each one. First, create a few entries that look like this in your journal, leaving space to write. (We'll cover what each of these means next.)

- Role
- Description
- Action

First, list the roles you currently have. Think about the roles you play:

- at work or at school
- in your family
- in your intimate relationships
- with your friends
- with your neighbors

Here's one example of a role: dutiful daughter. The process of writing this down can help you better understand that the role you are playing is just that—a role. It's not you.

Second, write a description of how you play each role. Continuing the example from above, you might say: *It started with trying to be who I thought my dad wanted me to be. But I notice that this role tends to spill over into other relationships, especially my relationships with men.*

Third, go down your list and consider which roles are still serving you, and which aren't. Which ones are you attached to? Those probably need to go. Mark off with a checkmark or star the roles which are no longer serving you.

Finally, decide what action you want to take regarding each role. For example, you might say: I want to shift the energy of this role to being loyal to myself and speaking my truth with respect and love to those around me. There is no right or wrong answer. The point of the exercise is to recognize the roles and release any that are no longer serving you.

Here are a couple more examples:

Role: Manager

Description: I was hired to manage a large team of people and look at the best ways to be efficient and responsive to our customers. I'm a good manager and good in the role, but I see that I've also taken responsibility for everyone's problems instead of empowering them to be responsible.

Action: I want to lighten up on the role of "managing" through control and start being an "inspirer." I'm also going to take the manager hat off when I leave work.

Role: Mother

Description: Mom to two small boys, ages four and seven. I feel exhausted and like I don't have a life outside of being a mom. Think I'm trying to be the perfect mom, whatever that is!

Action: I'm going to remember I'm a woman first, and a mom second. I'll set up someone to watch the kids for a couple of hours so I can spend some time by myself. I'll try to be the best mom I can be while giving myself more space. I'll stop defining myself as just a mom when I talk to myself or others.

This is the truth: you are not any of these identities; they are simply the roles, or masks, that you have taken on. No matter how much you love or hate the role, or how firm the mask is, the role is not the totality of you. You are the changeless force beneath the masks, the divine presence that makes the mask possible. Knowing this is the wisdom of the Warrior Goddess.

As you go beneath these different identities to the core of you, find the essence that has remained stable through each identity. Can you find the seed of your light beneath the roles? Go back to who you were before any roles, when you were a small child. What do you notice? Remember fully experiencing something without thought or reflection or judgment? These are the moments when there is no role, no narrator of who you should be, no regard for what others think. These are the moments of you being you, fully.

In the next section you'll learn an interesting paradox: One way to release the roles that no longer serve you is by choosing the new myth you want to embody.

The Power of Myth

Humans have been telling stories since the beginning. And myths, which teach an important ideal or concept, help us explain or otherwise make sense of the world around us. We are constantly writing myths about ourselves and others, often without realizing it, and one of the arts of the Warrior Goddess is her willingness to create her own mythology. Claiming your Warrior Goddess path means *choosing* what myth you want to play with, a myth that nourishes you and keeps you energized.

In this section, we will experiment with two types of myths, the big and the little. A big myth gives you sacred context; a little myth gives you focus.

Your Big Myth

Your big myth is the big picture for how and why your unique, precious Warrior Goddess light arrived on the planet.

Dreaming your big myth is first and foremost about outrageous, fabulous, expansive imagination. Go big. Be the heroine of your own story. Have a great support team. Give yourself superpowers.

The possibilities are endless:

- I am an angel finding her wings again.
- I am a warrior of light, sent by my tribe to explore planet Earth.
- I am a messenger of faith, here to share my heart and scatter seeds of love everywhere I go.
- I bring peace and connection from the very center of the Universe.

Pick a big myth that makes you glow. Forget sensible or practical or real. Make it big, magic medicine that you incarnated with. Choose your big myth consciously, but hold it lightly; do not get attached! It is a robe to wear, not your true self. Your essence cannot be defined or limited.

My bigger myth is that I am a daughter of the Goddess. My Goddess mother loves me fiercely, and always supports and holds me energetically. I am in service to her and my brothers and sisters, from minerals to plants to people. When I feel this myth my whole body relaxes, and I feel inspired, loved, and loving. I feel happy and confident.

When I get triggered by an external event and find myself reverting to the old identity of a shunned, awkward teenager, I remember I have a choice. Do I want to continue to hold this old image of myself as a gawky teenager, or do I want to make a new choice and be a daughter of the Goddess? As a daughter of the Goddess, I then can love that gawky teenager part of myself and see her good qualities: innocence, curiosity, inner joy. She is also a daughter, and a friend. I see her beauty rather than embodying her pain and awkwardness.

A word of caution: When you claim this big myth, all of your other identities will likely begin to clamor for attention. Your judge may say, "Oh, that is not true! You suck! You are weak!" Your victim may say, "Well, if you are an angel, then why are we struggling so much? Why won't someone take care of us? Where is my angel soul mate? Why do I have to work?" Smile at them. Giggle, don't struggle. Slip past the voices and keep claiming your big myth as truth.

You may need to come back to your big myth many times a day on some days. When you make a mistake and your judge or victim starts in, instead of listening and punishing yourself, you can say, "Hey, I am a daughter of the Goddess. I am an angel come to bring joy into the world. And I just made a mistake. I am learning about being human." And then explore what you could have done differently. What did you learn that you could put into action the next time a similar situation happens?

We always have the choice to review any action and gain insights and information so that our next actions come from more integrity and consciousness. Your big myth can help you access this energy. But it will not happen automatically. Be curious about and do the work needed to unweave the old, stuck places within by using the tools from previous Warrior Goddess chapters. It is only when we stop and lovingly go deeper into our actions and reactions that we digest and embody the lessons.

Holding a big myth allows you to be honest and creative about assessing and cleaning up mistakes. Do angels get punished? Would the Goddess beat you for bouncing your checkbook, or losing your job, or having an affair? Would She say to you, "See, you made the same mistake again—you should go back to sleep. Maybe if you hide from it something will change." No! But from the place of your big myth, you can see what changes you would like to make without beating yourself up.

Once you have a big myth to play with, you can dream up a little myth: a current definition (or several!) of yourself as a spark for growth.

Your Little Myth

If your big myth is the big picture for how and why you arrived on the planet, your little myth is the window you choose to shine that light through in your day-to-day life. Imagine that tomorrow when you wake up and go to your closet, along with your clothes there is also a new box marked "little myths." When you open it, there are outfits of various styles and colors, all marked with a role to experiment with. You can put these on and take them off as much as you'd like.

Your little myth is like a really fabulous outfit. It's a conscious choice of what persona or role you want to explore in your daily life.

Dig through the box and find the perfect outfit for what you want to create at this particular time of your life. What energy are you wanting to bring through into the world?

Here are some little myth roles you could try on: artist, healer, student, teacher, lover, mother, friend, employer, employee, coworker.

Don't pick just the roles you are most familiar with. The key to using your little myth to support your growth is to not base it on what society or the critics or your friends think you should be (or who you believe they want you to be). Instead ask: What little myth would best serve me now? What action do I want to support myself in taking at this time? What window do I want to shine my light through?

While your big myth is fantastical, your little myths are practical and simple.

What you are going for in a little myth is a framework that reminds you who you want to be. So when you wake up in the morning, you know why you are here (big myth) *and* you know what your focus for the day is (little myth).

Then when the distractions of the day begin, you will have more power to make choices. Whenever you ask yourself, "Should I do this or this?" refer back to your little myth. What would your little myth do?

For example, when I first explored a little myth for myself many years ago, I chose writer. At the time I was more a writer in my head than on paper. I used the little myth of "I am a writer" to help me step into both the feeling of the role and the action of it. When I put on my imaginary writer outfit, I gave myself the boost I needed to make choices to support myself in doing something I really wanted to do, but never quite seemed to get to.

Use your little myth as a way to identify, create, and fulfill your current life purpose. Your little myth will change throughout your life, as you may be a student for a while, then a mother, a teacher, or an artist. You can also have more than one little myth at a time. Just make sure that the little myth or myths you choose are where you want to go, not where you have been. Then your little myth will help break old, stagnant roles.

And remember, you get to define what your little myth represents. For example, choosing to explore the little myth of mother does not mean you have to be a biological mother. What are you consciously mothering? Someone recently asked me, "Have you had children yet?" My response was, "I'm full with mothering books." Shining your light fully into the world means fully claiming your unique Warrior Goddess manifestation. Consciously choosing a little myth can help you expand to your edges, claim your space, and move in a direction that serves your highest good.

As a Warrior Goddess, you know that both the big and little myths are ultimately just that—myths. The real you is much, much greater than what can be encapsulated in any story. And consciously choosing which myths you want to create rather than accepting the stories that were created for you is what being a Warrior Goddess is all about.

Have fun! Don't worry about creating the perfect little myth, or the most powerful big myth. Try them on. Take them off. Try something else on. And remember, you are not your big or little myth. You are the magic behind the myth, the wonder of life manifesting into form. And it is in the space of mystery where the biggest transformations happen.

Helping Others Heal

Years ago, after taking many groups to the pyramids of Teotihuacan in Mexico, a friend and I had a beautiful vision of
bringing an all-women's group on a pilgrimage to Teotihuacan.
Our intent was to connect with the female ancestors of this
ancient Toltec site, and open up to how we could be in service
to humanity.

The experience we had on our final day of this trip, at the
top of the majestic pyramid of the sun, transformed not just
our little group but rippled out to heal others in an unexpected
way. What happened that day also helped all of us to shed old
insecurities.

On our way up the pyramid we stopped and blessed each
cardinal direction, and left offerings of water and cornmeal
to honor the ancestors and creators of this sacred place. Pure,
sweet silence and prayers. As we moved up the pyramid, we
each became more unified and aligned with this peaceful energy.
But when we arrived at the top, my mind kicked back in. "Oh.
Lots of people in the center. Sunday. Busy. We will need to do
a quick ceremony."

I have had a couple prior experiences at Teotihuacan where
the crowds were upset at us for taking up the center to do a ceremony like the one we were about to perform. Most of the time
people ignore us, and I had held on to "people will be upset,"
which caused me to want to rush the ceremony.

As we came closer to the center, a small window of space
opened up in the crowd and I thought, "Well, we will do the
ceremony here quickly, and then move it to where there are
fewer people." In my vision earlier in the day I knew that Jill
would be across from me, and Diana and Kristi across from
each other. As the four of us sat down, the crowd continued

moving all around us, seemingly oblivious to our presence. "Don't bother getting too comfortable," I said, "we will not be here for long!"

I began the ceremony by saying, "Inside circle, look into each others' eyes. Outside circle, hold." We took three deep breaths, and I felt the energy of the inner circle lock in place and it seemed like time shifted from rushing forward to a place of being in the eternal present moment. Although I could feel this amazing power and energy coming from inside the circle, I was still nervous about what was happening outside our group. I glanced quickly around and my body flooded with relief and joy. People were actually circling us with curiosity and positive energy, totally open to what we were doing. We were being completely supported by strangers.

My expectation and fears were further blasted out of my being as I looked up and saw people with tears in their eyes, and others with their arms up, feeling the energy we were creating. I smiled to Jill and said to the group, "OK, you can get comfortable. We'll be here for a while." As I settled into gazing into Jill's eyes, I felt our circle nuzzle in closer and drop deeper into the electrifying energy of the moment.

I felt us as one organism, pure energy moving. I invited Diana and Kristi to pull out the chalice and water we had brought. It was as if the chalice and water just appeared in their hands; the energy did not shift at all. I knew there was something much, much bigger at work now. Instinctually Diana held out the chalice, and their hands met as Kristi poured the water and they both sent out healing energy of light and love.

"Now bring it up to the sky," I whispered, and they lifted the chalice up, letting the sun pour into it. I felt as if the energy was now peaking all around us, rushing from the bottom of the pyramid up into the chalice as a ray of light came down from the sky. "Pour a little onto the pyramid." So much emotion and tears of joy as the water flowed over the stone. We sat for a bit longer, bathing in the glow of energy. I dipped my fingers in the water and blessed each woman in our circle, touching water to her third eye.

Tears still come to my eyes now when I feel what happened next. A voice within me said, "Now share this with the people." I turned to Diana and said, "Let's stand up and share the water with everyone." She started blessing the crowd, and women began reaching out to her. Mothers held out their babies to be blessed. Young girls held out their jewelry. A Japanese woman reached out to be blessed and then gathered water in her hands for her husband, who was videoing everything. I encouraged Kristi to stand up as well, and soon I saw they needed more help, so I stood up as well.

Young boys, older women, grown men, all came with hands out, respectful, in awe, open. I scooped water into my hands over and over and turned to the crowd, pouring water into their hands, touching their foreheads. Women took water from my hands and carried it to their children. One woman was crying and thanking us over and over again. A man asked me, "What are you doing?" "We are blessing the water of Teotihuacan," I replied, and he nodded and said, "Thank you."

I stepped out of the circle and watched Diana and Kristi surrounded by people, our women's circle mingling with beloved strangers. Then Kristi was at my side, watching. She whispered, "Now pour the water on the pyramid." And a moment later Diana knelt down and emptied the chalice onto the pyramid. As she came over to us the crowd closed, reaching to touch the water. Our circle gathered around, and Diana pulled out flowers we had brought for the ceremony. We started passing them out to the circle, and immediately people came to take offerings as well. The crowd had become our new friends. By this time there were so many layers of people trying to touch the water that it was impossible to bring a final flower offering to the center of the pyramid.

We walked around the outside of the pyramid and blessed each direction with water and our flowers. At the second corner a tour guide stood with two clients, and one of them asked, "What are they doing?" The tour guide scoffed, and said, "I do not know, and they probably do not know either." My heart flew open! Yes! We do not know what we are doing! And we are being completely, utterly guided.

And the guidance is this: As Warrior Goddess women, we can bring healing back to the planet and the people. We must be brave, open, trusting, and giving. We need to move past old stories of being ladylike or nonthreatening or normal and break the chains of our fears to share our gifts fully. The world is waiting with open hands. It is time to stop isolating ourselves. It is time to step up to serve all.

Be the woman that you are meant to be. Not the woman you think you should be, or the woman others want you to be. Look in the mirror and say hello to the Warrior Goddess staring back at you. Befriend her. Support her. Love her. And let her open her wings to soar.

When you open your heart to yourself, quirks and all, you change the world. When you let go of pleasing others because you think you have to, when you relinquish trying to squeeze yourself into a metaphoric shoe that doesn't fit so you can be accepted, you come home to the comfort of yourself. And when you embrace the precious Warrior Goddess that you are, you naturally want others to know the truth of themselves as well. Each step in your healing, no matter how tiny, ripples out to heal everyone around you. And every time you embrace your fiery nature or your sweet stillness, every time you deliver a full-bodied yes or a clear no, also makes waves.

The world needs your brand of kindness and love, your power, your sacred ritual, your creativity, your quiet presence, your magnificent vision, your charming silliness.

Here's to you, Warrior Goddess: embodied heroine, slayer of unconsciousness, beloved of the world. Go forth and empower.

Epilogue

I found God in myself and I loved her . . .
I loved her fiercely.

—Ntozake Shange

As I woke up this morning from a dream, I thought of you. I imagined sitting across from you, Warrior Goddess to Warrior Goddess, holding both your hands in mine, looking into your eyes, and saying, "I believe in you. I see your beauty. I see your gifts. I have faith in you."

Even though I may not know you personally, I know you are worthy of love. I know you are a gift to humanity. And I know you probably need a dedicated cheerleader, a loving advocate. I know there are times when maybe you should not take yourself so darn seriously. I know, without a doubt, that you are important and valuable. I know you are me, and I am you. We are healing, growing, loving, falling down, getting back up again. We are women. We are a force that can change the world.

In my dream all women recognize their worth, their wisdom, the healing power of their laughter. We hold hands across nations, across religions, across divisions. And we reach out to invite every child, every man, every single being regardless of gender or belief or experience to hold hands with us. We weave a web of acceptance, respect, love, forgiveness.

And then we get to work celebrating life, dancing through our fears, and nurturing the sassy spark within each of us.

Be a Warrior Goddess. Keep cleaning, keep living the Warrior Goddess lessons. Commit to You. Align with Life. Purify Your Vessel. Ground Your Being and Free Your Past. Energize Your Sexuality and Creativity. Claim Your Strength and Ignite Your Will. Open Your Heart. Speak Your Truth. Embody Your Wisdom. Choose Your Path. Repeat.

Keep saying yes to yourself and let the nectar of your yes overflow so others can find their unique, divine yes. Be an inspiration. Be yourself.

Acknowledgments

My life overflows with an abundance of people to thank and share my immense gratitude for. Many beings through the years have inspired, nourished, and challenged me to become a Warrior Goddess. Here are some of the "families" I am blessed to be part of:

To the Ruiz family and team, my family of the heart: don Miguel Ruiz, don Miguel Ruiz Jr., Susan Ruiz, Jose Luis Ruiz, Coco, Gaya, Raquel, Karla, Eva. You are incredible lights. There are no words for the depth of my gratitude to you and your love, don Miguel. And a special high five to all the Toltec teachers who apprenticed with me under don Miguel. I love you all so much.

To my incredible publisher, Randy Davila and the Hierophant/Insight Events family: Jacob Norby, Allison Jacobs, Kim Coley, Rachel Davila, and editor Susie Pitzen. Randy, thanks for believing in me. Many years ago I prayed for someone in the publishing world who would see my writing potential and help nurture me to bring it forward. You have done this and so much more.

To the Toci—Toltec Center of Creative Intent—core team family (aka Sparkly Pants): Diana Adkins, Mary Adams, Shiila Safer, Coral Nunnery, Monique Barrow, Ben Barrow, Dan Gauthier, Keely Hamilton, Kerri Hummingbird, and Mary Nicosia, I love growing Toci with you. To friends/Toltec family/Thirteen Moons supporters: Lorri Rivers, Ceci Zuniga, Laura Toups, Deborah Williams, Walker Mencia, Jewel Lotus, Angela Murphy, Brenda Lee Gauthier, Diana Spicer, Tammy Shotwell, Kara Watson, Katherine Daniels, Nikko Bivens, September Scheldrup, Radha Bhrid Ghain, Sloan Christagau, Marilyn Brown, Maya Adjani, Yonatan Hoffman, Suzanne McBride, Stephanie Lowe, River Menks, Stephen Seigel, Karen Wecker, Jai Cross, Cindy McPherson, Kevin Flores, Trisha McWaters, RMaya Briel, Mark Kuhlman, River del Llano, Nikki Davis, and Gabriel Haaland.

To all listed here, and many who are not, this acknowledgment would be pages long if I shared what is in my heart for each of you. There are so many more in the Toci family, and I send you all my love for being part of such a beautiful dream of community and healing with me.

To my Sundoor tribe: Peggy Dylan, thank you for holding the fire of your heart so powerfully that you shine on so many. Gratitude to Cindy Bond, Steve Brougher, Taya Stanley, Barbara Briner, Steve and Vicki Mulhearn, and all the firewalk instructors and dancers around the planet.

To my Wisdom/Ubiquity/Earth Tribe cocreators and dear friends Judith Yost and Will Taegel: You continually amaze me. Gratitude to all Wisdom graduate school teachers and students for merging heart and body with intellect.

To my female mentors: Vicki Noble and Cerridwyn Fallingstar, the first two teachers who lit a fire in my heart for the Goddess. To Ana Forrest and the Forrest Yoga family for kicking my butt in the best way possible through teacher training and beyond. Ana, gratitude for your abiding friendship and support. To Janet Mills for believing in me and guiding me. I'm so happy to be part of growing the Four Agreements dream with you and the Amber-Allen Publishing family. To Gini Gentry, thank you for your sacred mirroring and humor. Sarah Rose Marshank, thank you for your fierce love and for being such a magical sister/mentor/friend. Audrey Lehmann, gratitude for our enduring friendship. Diana Adkins, thank you for your amazing, loving support of me and Toci.

To my core family: my mom, Maggie Gaudet, and my sister, Christy Gaudet, for always being such amazing cheerleaders. You are the best family ever! To T, for standing by me through so much, making me laugh, and being as adventurous as I am. Here's to many more magical creations in the kitchen, the garden, and beyond. To my Davis Goddess sisters family: Autumn, Isis, Saurin, Heather, Aimee, and Jesikah. Thanks for loving me no matter what. To my godchildren, Rowan, Nash, Kyra, and Amara. You bring hope and joy to my heart.

Finally, thank you to all the beings over the years who have been part of the Thirteen Moons circles across the globe. This book is really for you, inspired by you. Thanks to you for reading this book, dear reader: Welcome to the Warrior Goddess family. I'm grateful for your courage, your willingness, and your unique fabulousness. Shine on!

Further Reading

There are so many beautiful, empowering books for women. Here is a small sampling of some of my favorite women authors sorted by chapter. Share your favorites with us at:

http://www.facebook.com/warriorgoddesswomen

Introduction: Live Your Warrior Goddess Greatness

When God Was a Woman by Merlin Stone

The Chalice and the Blade: Our History, Our Future by Riane Eisler

Warrior Women: An Archaeologist's Search for History's Hidden Heroines by Jeannine Davis-Kimball and Mona Behan

Lesson One: Commit to You

The Places That Scare You: A Guide to Fearlessness in Difficult Times by Pema Chödrön

Fierce Medicine: Breakthrough Practices to Heal the Body and Ignite the Spirit by Ana T. Forrest

Femme Vital! by Peggy Dylan

Lesson Two: Align with Life

The Spiral Dance: A Rebirth of the Ancient Religion of the Goddess by Starhawk

Finding Your Way in a Wild New World: Reclaim Your True Nature to Create the Life You Want by Martha Beck

There Is Nothing Wrong With You: Going Beyond Self-Hate by Cheri Huber

Broken Open: How Difficult Times Can Help Us Grow by Elizabeth Lesser

Lesson Three: Purify Your Vessel

Shakti Woman: Feeling Our Fire, Healing Our World—The New Female Shamanism by Vicki Noble

Clear Your Clutter with Feng Shui by Karen Kingston

Your Spacious Self: Clear the Clutter and Discover Who You Are by Stephanie Bennett Vogt

Lesson Four: Ground Your Being and Free Your Past

The Wounded Woman: Healing the Father-Daughter Relationship by Linda Schierse Leonard

Daughters and Mothers: Making It Work by Julie Firman and Dorothy Firman

Radical Acceptance: Embracing Your Life with the Heart of a Buddha by Tara Brach

Lesson Five: Energize Your Sexuality and Creativity

Sex for One: The Joy of Selfloving by Betty Dodson

Aphrodite's Daughters: Women's Sexual Stories and the Journey of the Soul by Jalaja Bonheim

Better Than I Ever Expected: Straight Talk About Sex After Sixty by Joan Price

Lesson Six: Claim Your Strength and Ignite Your Will

Revolution from Within: A Book of Self-Esteem by Gloria Steinem

Lean In: Women, Work, and the Will to Lead by Sheryl Sandberg

Dancing in the Flames: The Dark Goddess in the Transformation of Consciousness by Marion Woodman and Elinor Dickson

Lesson Seven: Open Your Heart

Love for No Reason: 7 Steps to Creating a Life of Unconditional Love by Marci Shimoff

A Heart as Wide as the World by Sharon Salzberg

Belonging Here: A Guide for the Spiritually Sensitive Person by Judith Blackstone

Lesson Eight: Speak Your Truth

The Dance of Connection: How to Talk to Someone When You're Mad, Hurt, Scared, Frustrated, Insulted, Betrayed, or Desperate by Harriet Lerner

Daring Greatly: How the Courage to Be Vulnerable Transforms the Way We Live, Love, Parent, and Lead by Brené Brown

Everything Is Workable: A Zen Approach to Conflict Resolution by Diane Musho Hamilton

Lesson Nine: Embody Your Wisdom

Discover Your Psychic Type: Developing and Using Your Natural Intuition by Sherrie Dillard

The New Feminine Brain: Developing Your Intuitive Genius by Mona Lisa Schulz

The Purpose of Your Life by Carol Adrienne

Lesson Ten: Choose Your Path

The Four-Fold Way: Walking the Path of the Warrior, Teacher, Healer and Visionary by Angeles Arrien

A Mythic Life: Learning to Live Our Greater Story by Jean Houston

Wisdom's Choice: Guiding Principles from the Source of Life by Kathryn Adams Shapiro

Resources

Visit the Warrior Goddess website and get additional resources at:

www.warriorgoddess.com

Look for the *Warrior Goddess Training* book link on the front page and use the password "WGTBR" to get access to all the bonus material.

Like the Warrior Goddess Facebook page and get daily inspiration at:

www.facebook.com/warriorgoddesswomen

Join my Warrior Goddess Training global circle via the Web and phone. For more information visit:

www.warriorgoddess.com

About the Author

HeatherAsh Amara is the founder of Toci—the Toltec Center of Creative Intent and the author of *The Toltec Path of Transformation: Embracing the Four Elements of Change* and *No Mistakes!: How You Can Change Adversity into Abundance*. She is dedicated to supporting women and men in becoming more curious, open, courageous, humorous, creative, loving, accepting, and impeccable explorers of their truth. She lives in Austin, Texas, and travels extensively. Visit her at www.heatherashamara.com.

books that inspire your body, mind, and spirit

Hierophant Publishing
8301 Broadway, Suite 219
San Antonio, TX 78209
888-800-4240

www.hierophantpublishing.com